Experiencing God in
THE HIDDEN PLACE

A Journey of Hope and Healing

Vickie Bennett

WestBow
PRESS®
A DIVISION OF THOMAS NELSON
& ZONDERVAN

Copyright © 2020 Vickie Bennett.

All rights reserved. No part of this book may be used or reproduced by any means, graphic, electronic, or mechanical, including photocopying, recording, taping or by any information storage retrieval system without the written permission of the author except in the case of brief quotations embodied in critical articles and reviews.

This book is a work of non-fiction. Unless otherwise noted, the author and the publisher make no explicit guarantees as to the accuracy of the information contained in this book and in some cases, names of people and places have been altered to protect their privacy.

WestBow Press books may be ordered through booksellers or by contacting:

WestBow Press
A Division of Thomas Nelson & Zondervan
1663 Liberty Drive
Bloomington, IN 47403
www.westbowpress.com
1 (866) 928-1240

Because of the dynamic nature of the Internet, any web addresses or links contained in this book may have changed since publication and may no longer be valid. The views expressed in this work are solely those of the author and do not necessarily reflect the views of the publisher, and the publisher hereby disclaims any responsibility for them.

Author photo: Melissa Jurasovich Photography
Cover art work: Andrew Wesley Bennett

ISBN: 978-1-9736-8650-7 (sc)
ISBN: 978-1-9736-8651-4 (hc)
ISBN: 978-1-9736-8649-1 (e)

Library of Congress Control Number: 2020903527

Print information available on the last page.

WestBow Press rev. date: 03/12/2020

All Scripture quotations, unless otherwise indicated, are taken from the Holy Bible, New International Version®, NIV®. Copyright ©1973, 1978, 1984, 2011 by Biblica, Inc.™ Used by permission of Zondervan. All rights reserved worldwide. www.zondervan.com The "NIV" and "New International Version" are trademarks registered in the United States Patent and Trademark Office by Biblica, Inc.™

Scripture quotations marked (GNT) are from the Good News Translation in Today's English Version- Second Edition Copyright © 1992 by American Bible Society. Used by Permission.

Scripture quotations marked (CEV) are from the Contemporary English Version Copyright © 1991, 1992, 1995 by American Bible Society, Used by Permission.

Scripture marked (NCV) taken from the New Century Version®. Copyright © 2005 by Thomas Nelson. Used by permission. All rights reserved.

Scripture quotations marked (NLV) are taken from the New Life Version, copyright © 1969 and 2003. Used by permission of Barbour Publishing, Inc., Uhrichsville, Ohio 44683. All rights reserved.

Scripture marked (KJV) taken from the King James Version of the Bible.

"From one woman's story of suffering, we peer into an entire nation's suffering. With heartbreakingly haunting images, Vickie offers a raw view of China's orphanage system as well as a raw view of her own faith from the heights to the depths. She provides the reader a compelling and gripping invitation to journey deeper into the soul and meet God. You will not be the same after reading this book."
~Dr. Tammy L. Smith
National and International Speaker
Author, "*Soul Healing*" and "*Soul Satisfaction*"

"Vickie is a faith warrior like none I've ever known. I was moved by her candor as she wrestled with God, faith and the innumerable questions we all face when our hope is destroyed. On these pages, you will find grace, healing and a God who breathes faith into the darkest of places."
~Alison Hooper, Editor and Co-Author, "*Soul Hearted*"

"*The Hidden Place* is a beautifully written story of one woman's journey through the joys and challenges of following God's call. In this book, you will experience Vickie's heartfelt vulnerability and authenticity as she shares the excitement of the birth of a vision, the pain of the death of the vision, and the deep growth that comes from renewal and restoration."
~Jayne Schooler
Author, "*Wounded Children, Healing Homes*"

Contents

Dedications from Vickie: xi

Chapter 1 The Beginning 1
Chapter 2 The Return 9
Chapter 3 The Invisible Children 17
Chapter 4 Lucy And Mary 27
Chapter 5 The Big Yes 38
Chapter 6 Mimi 43
Chapter 7 He Gives And Takes Away 56
Chapter 8 The Horrible Day 64
Chapter 9 The Long Journey Back 76
Chapter 10 The Battle 85
Chapter 11 From Undone To Unglued 90
Chapter 12 Lament 99
Chapter 13 Entering The Hidden Place 108
Chapter 14 Weariness And Whispers 112
Chapter 15 Healing Through Tears 117
Chapter 16 The Soil Of My Soul 122
Chapter 17 The Cobwebs 130
Chapter 18 Half-Truths And Collateral Damage 135
Chapter 19 The Great Reveal 141
Chapter 20 Leaving The Hidden Place 148

Endnotes 163
About the Author 165

Dedications from Vickie:

To my husband Jim—I love you and I thank God for you every single day. You are my best friend and my greatest supporter. You are my rock. Thank you for holding me up when I didn't have the strength to do it myself. Thank you for allowing me the time away to be alone with God as we wrote this book together. Thank you for always loving me unconditionally and being such an example to our children of what true covenant looks like.

To our children Adam, Andrew, and Amber—Thank you for your love and support despite having your parents leave to live on the other side of the world. You selflessly cheered us on and never once complained about sharing us with so many other children in China. We love you all and are so proud of you!

To our children Austin, Abraham, Anagrace, and Amelia—Thank you for serving alongside of us. Never once did you complain. You served the babies every single day, giving them your whole hearts with unconditional love. You sacrificed the luxuries of living in America to serve the orphans in China. Never forget the lessons God taught you of loving, serving, and giving to others in need.

To our parents, our siblings, and our families—We were told that many missionaries receive resistance and discouragement from those closest to them. That was never the case for us. Your support, prayers, and encouragement were life-giving. We know it was not easy having us so far away. Thank you for honoring our calling to serve the orphans in China.

To my fellow board members: Hilary, Huang Ying, Kimberley, Susan, Suzanne, and Valerie. You ladies are true warriors in every sense of the word. You held my arms up when I no longer could. You loved me, encouraged me, and supported me. You called me the dreamer, yet you never discouraged me from dreaming of what could be. Then you helped us find a way to make those dreams come true. You are, and forever will be, my kindred spirits and Sisters in Christ. I love you all so deeply!

To Tammy—you are more than a counselor, you are my friend. Thank you for all your words of wisdom. Your sensitivity to the Holy Spirit as He guides you through my healing journey. We've shared so many tender moments, as well as a few laughs along the way. What a ride it has been! There is no doubt God placed you in my life. You are my hero!

To Ali—my editor and newfound friend. Thank you for making my rambling words come together. For putting up with my terrible grammar and wordy sentences. For pushing me and challenging me every step of the way. What a pair we make!

To my son, Andrew—you took my vision for the cover of this book and breathed life into it. I am so grateful to have you be a part of this journey with me. I am so proud of you and all the hard work you have put into becoming such a gifted artist. Thank you for using your gift for God's kingdom work.

To Kimberley—Whew! Girlfriend, where would I be without you and your tender soul. When I was left so wounded coming off the battlefield. You dropped whatever you were doing to come to my rescue. Whether it was to dry my tears, lift me up in prayer, give me a sturdy shoulder to lean on or cheer me on in my writing. You declared many years ago God would use this story for His Glory. Now here we are! Thank you for believing in me and being such a faithful and loyal friend. I love you, sweet friend!

To our faithful Grace Village volunteers: Emily, Rebecca, Erin, and Ashley. You are the epitome of our Father's hands and feet. It was a privilege to serve on the front lines with you. What a beautiful group of selfless servants you all are! Thank you for helping make Grace Village a loving home for all our children.

To our donors and volunteers—You served and gave donations for more than a decade towards our work in China. It really did take a village to care for all those precious children. The resources of donations and volunteer hours were crucial to the success of the programs, and to our ability to do what was needed to care for the hundreds and hundreds of children over the years. Thank you!

To our prayer warriors—You prayed for our family and our children so faithfully through the years. You were the heartbeat of our ministry. Thank you for loving us and supporting us. Giving us a safe place to land in our requests and spurring us on along the way.

Last, but certainly not least, I want to dedicate this book to all the orphans who are left behind in China. I pray for you daily. I am SO sorry for your suffering. Know that God sees you and that you are not forgotten. He loves you and so do we. You are cherished and you are chosen. You are HIS. Nothing, and no one, can ever snatch you from His Hands. It was truly an honor to be written into each of your stories.

A Note from Vickie:

When I first felt God nudging me to write this story, I remember so vividly all the thoughts and questions that rolled around in my mind.

Do I share about the hundreds of orphans we served in a communist country? Or do I share about my personal journey of deep grief and suffering?

I could sense God telling me it was to be both.

But how? I asked. How do I share a story with such contrasting themes?

God showed me a very clear picture—the parallel condition of the human heart and the indelible mark suffering leaves on it.

After serving over a decade inside an orphanage, beyond the physical images of the children's daily lives, I experienced firsthand the effects that suffering, neglect, and abuse had on them. Their hearts and minds were riddled with trauma, loneliness, hopelessness, fear, and rejection.

The same is true for each of us. Whether it's the death of a loved one, illness, betrayal, etc. These events leave our hearts and minds riddled with trauma, loneliness, hopelessness, fear, and rejection.

What God has taught me through my journey is that the effects of suffering do not discriminate. They are the same for a free person, or for an orphan who is imprisoned.

The human heart and mind were designed by God to be loved. When that love is violated in any way, it leaves a mark on us. A mark that if left unattended will have lasting effects on the human soul.

My prayer, as you move through the pages of this story, is that God will use it to accomplish His desires for your life. I pray, in expectation, that the same God who spoke the stars into being will ensure that this story is placed in the hands He wishes it to reach.

I pray you will feel His presence and experience Him in ways you never have before. Allow Him to hold you close as He whispers in His gentle voice His invitation to go away with Him to the Hidden Place.

Vickie

Chapter 1

The Beginning

I grew up on a farm in Ohio surrounded by acres of cornfields. I was the middle child with an older brother and a younger sister. Our parents had a loving marriage. We went to church every Sunday. Though we didn't have a lot of money, we were happy, and I had a wonderful childhood. By all accounts, I was just a simple country girl.

I graduated from high school and started my career as an accountant. I got married to my husband Jim, and we had three beautiful children. We went to church every Sunday. I read my Bible every day. I put my non-tithing check in the offering plate. We lived a seemingly uneventful life, focused on raising our kids and moving up our respective career ladders.

I loved God as best I knew how, and I knew that He loved me. Yet up to that point in my life, He was simply that—God. The religion I learned taught me that my invitation to accept Jesus as my personal savior assured me a spot in heaven for eternity. I was not taught the value of experiencing the Holy Spirit or having a personal relationship with Him. Not to mention, my prayer life was basically a one-sided conversation. I did all the talking, mostly running to God during times of need.

In all sincerity, I think back to my relationship with God at that time and I'm ashamed to admit just how shallow and self-centered I was. Rather than seeking God, I was always searching for what God could do for me. I had no idea who He was, and I certainly had no idea how deeply He really loved me. Because I never took the time to get to know Him, I lacked insight into how He was operating in my life. I simply went through the motions, checked all the boxes I believed a good Christian girl should, and went on with my daily life.

Fast forward about twenty years and Jim, our daughter and I were on the other side of the world preparing to pass through the gates of a communist orphanage in China.

Wait a minute, what? I know what you're thinking. How on earth did I go from the cornfields of Ohio to an orphanage in a third world country? Truth be told it started with my selfish desire to have another baby. I had recently turned forty years old; my two oldest sons were out of high school and our daughter was entering the ninth grade. Call it premature empty nest syndrome (I can assure you; such a thing does exist), but there I was nearing the next season of parenting with a deep desire for another baby.

After many conversations and much pleading, including prayers for God to change Jim's heart, Jim finally agreed to adopt a baby. Eleven months later we traveled to China to bring home a beautiful nine-month-old baby girl.

However, little did I know that God had a much greater agenda, and He decided to kick things into high gear starting with my request to change Jim's heart.

Before we left China, Jim announced that he wanted to adopt a second baby. Gulp! So, there we were, a little over a year after our first adoption, returning to China for our second trip. Before bringing home our second child, a son, we offered to return to our daughter's orphanage to deliver some donated items for the children there. We were told that this orphanage was closed to outside visitors. We expected that this visit would be short and sweet. We would not go inside, and we would simply smile and accept their gratitude. You can imagine our surprise when after handing over our donations, the orphanage director met us and asked if we'd like to see the orphanage. I immediately responded, "YES!" When she asked what we'd like to see, I blurted out, "The babies!"

We loaded into the elevator which took us to the eighth floor. We walked down the corridor and through a door that led us to three rooms, each room divided by a wall of glass. From where I stood, I could see all the way to the back of the third room. Each of the three rooms was filled with rows and rows of cribs.

The first thing that I noticed was the silence. You could have heard a pin drop. Everything was sterile and heavy, and the words that came to mind as I stood there were "silent prison."

At least one hundred cribs were lined up head to toe, row after row after row, all the way to the back wall of the third room. Throughout the three rooms, I spotted two or three nannies who appeared to be busily working, though they never spoke a word.

Despite it being early in the morning, I assumed from the silence that it was nap time. I slowly walked up to the first crib and peeked inside. Looking back at me was a baby with big beautiful almond eyes just like my daughter's. The baby was wide awake. I quickly looked down the row of cribs and realized that not only was each crib occupied, but all the babies were awake. I gasped and said, "Jim, look! They're all awake!"

I motioned to the Director, using gestures to ask if I could pick up the baby. She agreed. As I scooped up the baby, two things happened. First, I almost dropped her as she slowly started to fall backward out of my arms—she was unable to hold up her head even though she was at least six months old.

Second, I became overwhelmed by a smell. The baby's odor was a pure stench. Instead of a diaper, she had at least half a dozen filthy shop rags wrapped around her bottom and covered in plastic. The plastic was tied with what looked like a bungee cord. The smell of urine and filth nearly took my breath away. Jim and our teenage daughter who was with us also picked up babies to hold.

I don't know whether you've ever had something happen to you that you knew instantly would change your life. For me, this was that moment. My simple country-girl mind never knew that such injustice existed in the world. These children were literally warehoused, and to see it and touch it was profound. In that instant, something inside of me broke, and I was completely and utterly undone. It took everything in my power to fight back the tears. I had a huge lump in my throat. I was so afraid that if I cried it would make a scene, and the orphanage staff would ask us to leave. So, I took a deep breath and tried to gather my composure. I knew the Director didn't speak English, so I told Jim that we were not leaving the orphanage until we had touched and prayed over every baby in the nursery. That is exactly what we did.

As we moved throughout the rows of cribs, it became apparent that the babies were in order based on their age. The further down the rows we went, the older the babies appeared and the worse their conditions. By the time we arrived at the back of the room, the babies were lethargic

The Beginning

at best. They had sores and flat spots on their heads from laying in their cribs 24/7.

Their cribs were nothing more than metal bars with a wood board for a mattress. The babies barely responded to our voices, and they made little to no eye contact. At one point there were a few babies who appeared to be crying. Even though their mouths were open, we could not hear an audible noise. They were literally crying silent tears.

That day we held and prayed over a hundred babies. We were told that there were another hundred babies on the floor above us, though we never got to see them.

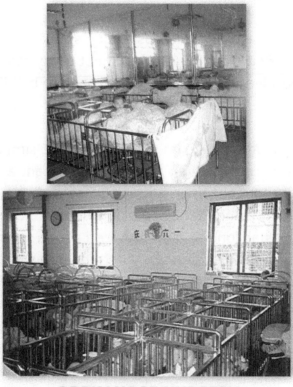

ORPHANAGE NURSERY

By the time we reached the back of the last room, we had worn out our welcome. The Director smiled as she graciously escorted us to the elevator. The taxi ride back to the hotel was silent as we tried to process what we had just witnessed.

That night I tossed and turned. I could not sleep. Every time I closed my eyes, I would see the faces of those precious babies. They haunted me. Once your eyes have seen such horror, it can never be unseen. Ever.

At around 2 am I finally gave up trying to sleep and moved over to the chair in our room. I sat there numb. I wanted to pray, but I didn't know what to say. Finally, the flood gates opened and all I could do was sit and cry. I sobbed and sobbed. I cried until there were no tears left inside of me. Then I just sat there in the dark. At that moment, a wave of righteous anger swelled up inside of me. Words flew from my heart and out of my mouth, "God, I have no idea how to help those babies, but if you will provide a way, I will do whatever you ask of me to help them."

Even though I had no idea what that simple prayer meant for me at the time, I knew that I meant every word of it; it was not spoken on a whim. I was certain with every particle of my being that I would do whatever I could to help those babies as long as God provided a way.

I'm not sure what brought you to hold this book in your hands. Maybe you are part of the adoption community, or maybe you have gone through a life-altering traumatic experience and someone suggested that you read this. Maybe you are a Christian or maybe you are not. Maybe you are not even sure if there is a God. I don't know what your personal situation is, but whatever the case may be, I want you to hear this. When my journey began over a decade ago, I was just your average person, and I still am today.

I have no special talents, and there is absolutely nothing

The Beginning

extraordinary about me. I am an accountant, a wife, and a mother, living a simple middle-class life. I am not a famous author, songwriter, or athlete. There is absolutely nothing extraordinary about me or my life. I was and still am just an ordinary girl.

Now I can assure you that I'm not trying to be all Humble Hazel. I share all of this because I believe that for most of you who are reading this, you can relate to what I'm saying. I grew up with a brother who was extremely gifted as an athlete. He was drafted out of high school by a professional baseball team. Then there was me (cough, cough). I knew I was a good person and I loved the family I was born into, but deep down inside I knew that I would never receive the kind of recognition that my brother received.

In sharing my story, many times I have thought, "Sure those people can tell their stories because they have happy endings. Look at their lives. They've written books, they speak to large audiences, they've recorded a number one song, they this and they that." I mention all this because the only reason I've walked the journey that I have this past decade is not that I had anything special to offer. Rather it's because I simply said "yes" to God.

When my journey of faith started, my heart was filled with nothing more than two selfish desires: 1) get what I could from God and 2) get to heaven. My faith, if that's what you even want to call it, was that plain and simple. That is exactly where my faith was when I sat in that hotel room on the other side of the world and gave God my yes. All I had wanted was another baby, but God had other plans. I had absolutely no clue what I was saying and what it would mean for me, but that simple yes was my starting point to a deeper and richer journey with God than I could have ever imagined.

My encouragement to you right now is to just sit back, relax and listen to my story. If you are here to learn more about our children who we served in China, I pray that they will not only touch your life, but that they will change you. If you're here because you're trying to find your way through a dark season in your life, please keep reading. As you will soon learn, I have been through difficult and dark seasons in which I didn't think I would survive. Promise me you'll stick with me. I have so much more to say to you as this story unfolds. Maybe you are at a point in your life where you don't trust anyone, including God, and that's okay. Keep reading and don't give up. I am confident God has something for you through the pages of this book.

Chapter 2
The Return

It had been eleven months since I sat in my hotel room and said "yes" to God in the middle of the night—eleven months since I told God that I would do whatever I could to help those babies. Eleven months from the moment I landed back in the US after our second adoption trip to China. Eleven months of sleepless nights as the images of the babies' suffering haunted my mind.

God had taken my "yes", and in those eleven months, He changed my heart. What started as a midlife journey to adopt a baby, turned into a midlife journey to adopt two babies. Eleven months after that second adoption, Jim and I were committed to serving orphans in China no matter what it required of us. God had started us on a path that would lead us to return to China to serve its many orphans.

The hope was this: we would return to China to start a program that would give the babies a loving and nurturing environment. We would train the staff to care for the babies in a way that would help them to develop on target. After an initial visit to China to set up the program, we would return stateside and serve in an ongoing capacity as administrators and fundraisers for the program.

With a plan in place, we started by contacting our

adoption agency. We asked them to help us take the first steps toward seeking permission to work inside the orphanage. We then completed the necessary paperwork to establish a US non-profit organization so that we could begin fundraising to support the work we would be doing in China.

Also, during that time, I reached out to several other mamas who had adopted children from this same orphanage. I knew that their daughters had come to them with many of the same developmental delays my daughter had. Delays which were a result of months of abuse and neglect they had endured while living in the orphanage. I hoped that after explaining to these mamas all that we had seen and experienced in the orphanage, it would become their passion and drive to want to help as well.

On top of everything God had been doing inside my heart during those eleven months, He was just as busy working to open China's communist doors for us to serve their orphans.

Sure enough, that is exactly what happened. God swung the doors wide open and we sprinted right through them. That was only the beginning of years and years' worth of favor and miracles from God as we began this new midlife journey!

Once we returned to China, we worked with other volunteers to create a program that provided nannies with training and education in basic infant care and early childhood development. We hired our own staff, the orphanage provided a designated room for our program, and within eleven months we had raised enough funds from generous donors to run the program for an entire year.

The adrenalin that was running through my system was full throttle as I returned to the very place that eleven

The Return

months earlier had broken my heart into pieces. Only this time I no longer felt helpless, rather I felt empowered.

God had provided the way, just as I had asked. With God ultimately providing the wisdom, knowledge, and resources, all I had to do was obey and follow.

Walking back into the nursery eleven months after that initial visit was surreal. Nothing had changed except that some of the babies were now a year older. Some had been adopted internationally and others had passed away, but still in front of me were the same number of rows and cribs filled with babies.

When one or two babies would leave, one or two more were abandoned and brought to the orphanage. In those early days, it was common to see several babies brought to the orphanage each week. Normally they were healthy baby girls. China's history led many families to abandon their daughters, sometimes for economic reasons. However, more often than not, abandoned baby girls were a result of China's one-child policy and the country's preference for boys over girls.

I cannot begin to tell you the questions I have been asked over the years about China - the country, its people, and especially the misconceptions related to China's orphan crisis.

First, why does the country favor boys, and why were most of the abandoned children girls? During the Mao administration (1949-1976), China implemented the infamous one-child policy. The intent was to help control, if not decrease, the imploding population of the country. While the policy did accomplish its intended goal, it unexpectedly resulted in a dramatic increase in orphans throughout the country, specifically girls.

At that time, China did not have a social security system

in place to care for the aging and retired. When individuals grew old, the family, specifically the son, was responsible for caring for them. Aging parents would live with their son and his respective family. If a family had a daughter who married, the daughter would care for her in-laws, leaving her parents to care for themselves.

Out of necessity, a great value was placed on sons over daughters. Because of the one-child policy, if a family had a girl then they were faced with the likely possibility of not having the provisions they would need to take care of themselves in their old age. In turn, many families chose to abandon their daughter in the hopes of having a future male child.

So then why abandon the baby and not give her up for adoption? Surrendering your child is not permitted in China. Therefore, if a family was forced with the decision to give up their child, abandonment was the only option.

Finally, why didn't families simply keep their first child if it was a girl and pay the government fine required to have a second child? Unfortunately, China's laws were not that cut and dry. Fines varied depending on where the family lived. Sometimes family members would lose their jobs. Sometimes they were charged fines that were so exuberant that they equaled a year's wages.

We even know families who chose to pay the fine, but the government continued to repeatedly demand more money from them. Sometimes it would be additional fees and sometimes the government would prohibit their additional children from attending school. China's government came up with various policies to extort the family and deter them from keeping more than one child.

Meanwhile, the population numbers in the orphanages exploded and the staff found themselves inundated with overcrowding and lack of funding. It's hard to understand the

The Return

conditions in which these orphans live, and it's sometimes easy to point fingers at the orphanage staff and directors themselves. However, those who work in the orphanages are trying to do the best they can with limited resources.

For the most part, I do not believe that orphanage staff intends to harm or neglect the children. They are trying their hardest to provide for the children's basic needs of food and shelter, however, they have little to no resources with which to succeed.

Now that we have our little history lesson out of the way, let's return to the orphanage.

The goal of our trip back to the orphanage was to train our new staff and to establish our infant nurture program. We were there for about three weeks, and it was one of the longest and hardest three weeks of my life.

Every mistake that could have been made, I made it. I had no idea what I was doing. I had zero experience with doing business in an eastern country, and I knew very little about Chinese culture. The nationals would smile at me when talking, and only later I learned that they absolutely could not stand me.

We spent hours negotiating different facets of the program, finally coming to an agreement, only to return the next day to learn they had changed their minds. "Why?" I'd ask. My translator would tell me that she wasn't sure why. It was maddening!

Not to mention it was at least 120 degrees with the heat index, and the elevator in the orphanage didn't work. Each day we had to schlep our supplies and equipment up eight flights of stairs in brutal heat. I asked if I could stay behind to work through my lunch break, only to later find out I had offended them because it is their custom to take a two-hour midday break to eat and nap.

Speaking of food, this was another area of conflicting cultures. The local cuisine often consisted of something I lovingly called "funny food."

During our adoption trips, our guides would take us to restaurants that served western-friendly food. However, during this trip, the orphanage directors took us to their favorite restaurants, often restaurants that served the "funny food" I tried very much to avoid. For instance, locals dined on every part of the animal, bird, fish or whatever else; nothing was left to waste.

When I tell you that they served everything, I mean they served everything. I was served lungs, brains, clotted blood, the head, the feet, the eyes, the reproductive parts, and the granddaddy of them all, a pig's hoof. Of course, we were given the customary chopsticks to eat these luscious delicacies, creating an even greater cultural challenge.

After our first meal and my obvious body language of total disgust, I was told that I had offended them because I snubbed their meals. Being the good girl that I am, I started eating what was put before me. I took small bites, mixed with lots and lots of white rice, and I flushed it all down with a whole lot of hot tea. Slowly, I pushed my way through each meal, struggling through each bite.

When I returned to our hotel room each evening, (thank you, Jesus, for our five-star hotel which my spoiled American body landed in each night), I would take the hottest shower my body could handle. I stood in the shower and cried my eyes out because I was so sick from the food and the heat. My body was completely red because of the intensity of the hot water, but I didn't care. Those hot showers were my place of escape that allowed me to release all that I had bottled up inside.

Toward the end of the trip, the day had finally come for

us to move the babies into their new room. One by one we picked them up out of their respective cribs, freeing them from their tiny individual prisons. Confinement and neglect were the only life they had ever known.

We took the babies to their new room that was decorated with beautiful butterflies. Unlike the orphanage's sterile and heavy aesthetic, the infant room was filled with soft blankets for cuddling and lots of toys for playing.

I cannot begin to tell you the joy that filled my heart that day. No matter how bad the past three weeks had been for me, in that moment everything was better. The price that we paid for their freedom was worth every single moment that I had suffered.

For record-keeping purposes, we decided to give each of the babies in our program an English name. It protected their identities on the paperwork (which we kept in the US), and it made pronouncing their names a whole lot easier.

On this first trip, there was one particular baby that caught my attention. We gave her the name Clara. Clara was so shy and so fearful. As soon as she would see us, she immediately started crying. She gave us this look as if to say, "What bus stop did you come from?" In her mind, we absolutely did not belong there. Clara was part of the first group of babies to enter our new program. We were told that she had some developmental delays and despite her age, she was not able to crawl, let alone walk.

Clara had a beautiful round face with chubby cheeks. Her eyes were a deep dark brown. Her expressions were unforgiving. Whenever I saw Clara, she studied my face for a minute and then she would burst into tears. Our staff worked with her to try to assess if she had an actual medical need in addition to her developmental delay.

At one point I remember walking past the nursery and

seeing several Chinese doctors giving Clara acupuncture as she laid on her stomach and cried. Clara had such a soft gentle spirit about her, and I was so happy to see her placed in our program so that she could grow and learn.

Once we returned to the States, we received monthly pictures of each baby in our program along with a development report of their progress. Clara's report was always the first one I checked. I eagerly hoped and prayed to see the box checked next to the milestone progression "crawling."

Month after month, that box remained unchecked. It became apparent that Clara did have a medical need that was preventing her from developing at a normal rate, and because of that, the file that allowed her to be adopted was never prepared.

Following our initial trip to China to start our program, members of our US team and I returned to the orphanage several times a year. These visits served as a check-in, and they allowed us to continue building relationships with the orphanage directors and staff. Oh, and for the record, we finally became good enough friends that we were able to ask them to please not serve us any more "funny food".

As time passed, the orphanage directors and staff considered us regular visitors. It filled my heart with joy when the staff and some of the older children from the orphanage would wave and run to greet us each time we walked through the orphanage gates. There was absolutely nothing that we did that warranted the success of our program and organization. It was all God. Only God has the power to change the hearts of man and a communist government. That was one of the first lessons that He taught me as I began this crazy journey with Him.

Chapter 3
The Invisible Children

About three years into our partnership with the orphanage (yes, now both sides considered themselves partners in taking care of the children—a total God thing!) we realized that not all the babies in our program would be adopted. This meant we needed to consider the next phase of providing for them. We needed a preschool program to serve the toddlers and preschoolers, likely something with the resources to care adequately for young children with special needs.

To plan for this new program, we decided to travel to China, taking with us a team of specialists. We included a special education teacher, a physical therapist and several nurses.

Before our trip, the orphanage supplied us with a list of the children we would be meeting, a list which included the children's ages and special needs. Almost every child was either labeled blind or autistic. Honestly, we had no idea what we were walking into.

We planned to have each of our specialists set up an individual station to assess each child and determine his or her actual need. We would use that information to guide us in the development of our preschool program.

Once at the orphanage, we were given access to a part

of the building we had never been allowed to visit. The elevator took us to the sixth floor, and when we stepped off the elevator, we encountered an accordion gate that remained locked. Behind that gate were dozens of children. All these children lived confined behind the locked gate on the sixth floor of the orphanage. Our translator yelled for the staff, "Ayi, Ayi!" The word "Ayi" (pronounced I-E) means "Auntie" in Chinese, but it is also used as a title for a caregiver. Out from one of the open doorways came the ayi along with what seemed like a never-ending flow of children.

Again, we had never been granted access to these children so I'm not sure what we expected, but I can assure you it wasn't what I encountered in front of us.

At least thirty children were hopping up and down in excitement as the ayi struggled to unlock the padlock. When the gate was opened the madness began. The children swarmed us, and they attached themselves to us as a bee attaches to its beehive.

As we followed the ayi down the hallway, we had to physically walk with two to three children clinging to each of our respective legs. It was absolute chaos.

The ayi led us to a room with several wooden bookshelves, all of which were empty. Filling most of the space in the room was a huge ball pit.

In an instant, the scene turned from chaos to madness. It was clear that these children never spent much time in this room. Some of them went for the ball pit and balls started flying everywhere, while others remained attached to our legs.

My team looked at me with the most pathetic look of helplessness. One of them said, "Vickie, what are we going to do?" I replied, "We're going to Plan B. I don't know what that is, but that's where we're going!"

We all started laughing because honestly if we didn't laugh the only thing left to do was cry. The teacher on our team suggested that we get out the 500-piece Lego set that we had brought. We dumped the Legos onto the floor while dodging the flying Legos, we started to build little Lego creations. Soon the children followed our lead and did the same.

We spent the morning observing the kids, and as my eyes started to scan the children's faces, I realized that none of these children were ours from the infant nurture program.

So then where did these children come from? It was as if these children were invisible during all our prior trips to the orphanage.

That wasn't the only thing I noticed. The children's behavior also caught my attention. They acted like wild animals. They hit, bit, spit, pulled hair, punched and scratched each other. If that wasn't bad enough, even though they were old enough to speak, they didn't. Instead, they grunted and made animalistic noises. They had their own type of language made up of illegible sounds and hand gestures.

Soon the morning ended, and it was time to go to lunch. As our team gathered with our translator, we started talking about what we had just witnessed.

Through our translator, we learned that these children were in the orphanage even before our baby program days. This meant that they had never been held, nurtured or loved in the ways that we had nurtured the babies in our program. When these children were babies, they laid in their cribs 24/7. They had never been taught how to be human.

Then when it seemed it couldn't get any worse, we learned that the caregivers assigned to them were girls who had grown up in the orphanage themselves, most of whom were deaf and mute—hence the reason the children didn't know how to speak.

After a lengthy discussion, I told the team, "Okay, it's time to come up with a plan. First, plans for a preschool are out the window. The first thing these children need to learn is how to be human. Second, they must be taught how to process and how to handle their emotions. And most importantly, they need to learn how to communicate."

The team gathered and revised their evaluation forms. We gave each of the children an English name, and we created a roster. The team did the best they could to evaluate each child's health and cognitive ability.

Several days into the trip, I walked by the big room where the children normally stayed. I noticed a crib sitting up against the wall and a small child sitting in it. I popped my head in the door to look. Imagine my surprise when the child sitting in the crib was Clara!

When I went to go pick her up, she immediately started crying. Yup, it was Clara alright. I was a stranger to her, and she was letting everyone on the floor know it.

Through our translator, I asked the staff a few questions about her, and they confirmed that she still was unable to walk or crawl. When the orphanage had moved her from the baby floor, the days of receiving love and playtime ended, and she was now sentenced once again to a life of prison in a crib.

The physical therapist on our team was able to find a wooden chair with wheels on it that was sitting unused. She used some old pieces of foam to fill in the sides and the back of the chair so that Clara could sit upright in it. This chair became the ticket to Clara's escape from her crib.

Starting that day forward, the ayi put Clara in the chair,

and one of the children wheeled Clara down the hall to our activity room. Clara was able to sit at the table with the other children and she would play and draw. Before the end of the first day, she was smiling and giggling. My heart could not hold all the happiness inside that I felt for Clara.

After this trip, we returned to the States and quickly began making plans for our next orphanage program. I knew that this program would be more than a preschool program. This was a project of hope for the children who had been hidden away and made invisible their entire lives.

We returned to the orphanage several months later and were able to take what was then an empty space and transform it into a beautiful preschool room. Thanks to a generous donor, we filled the room with desks, chairs, preschool supplies and bookcases full of learning toys. It was everything a preschool teacher could ever dream of. We hired three very special teachers and to date, the preschool program was by far one of the greatest success stories of our organization.

Our program was easily measured as a success, but at the end of the day, my heart was left wondering if it really was? Yes, our children were given the chance to laugh and to play and to learn and to grow, but the reality of their future was still the same. Regardless of how much better their experience was living in the orphanage, they were still orphans with little to no hope of ever being adopted by a family.

As for Clara, her shyness and fear slowly disappeared with each returning visit, however, the reality of her life remained hopeless. She was unable to walk - a child living with a disability and living in a Chinese orphanage.

Clara eventually grew out of the chair we made for her. Like the other children who could not walk, she resorted to army crawling to wherever she needed to go. Clara never seemed to mind, and she always had a smile on her face. Nevertheless, it was hard for me to watch the reality of her difficult everyday life.

CLARA IN MAKESHIFT CHAIR

CLARA IN PRESCHOOL

Something that was always hard for me to watch was when children like Clara who could not walk would have to drag themselves to the bathroom. The orphanage toilets were porcelain inserts in the floor. Being an orphanage full of young children, the floor surrounding the toilets was always covered in urine and whatever else. Because they cannot get themselves up to stand over the toilet like most people, they have to drag themselves through the muck to use the restroom.

My mind and my heart will never forget the smell of the children when we would hold them on our laps. The children rarely received baths, and when they did, soap was rarely used (despite our best efforts to train the staff). I loved holding Clara, and even though the smells from the uncleanliness were strong, I didn't mind. She was such a special little girl who deserved so much more than the life that had been given to her.

No matter how many trips I made to China and no matter how many days I spent with the children, it never got any easier. Every evening I returned to my hotel room and peeled off the clothes that were saturated in urine and filth.

Every evening I followed the same routine. I ran the shower as hot as I could physically tolerate, and I stood underneath it trying to wash away the sorrow and the grief that was bottled up inside my heart. There was not a single night that went by when I was in China, that I did not cry in the shower as I mourned for every child my hands had encountered that day.

After traveling back and forth to China so many times, people frequently asked me about the length of the flights and if the travel ever got any easier. From Ohio, we always traveled to a large city like Chicago or Washington DC and then connect to what I called our "big plane." From there, travel varied between 14-17 hours.

Did it ever get easier? Yes and no. I never minded the flights going over because I was always filled with so much adrenaline and anticipation, eager to see all our babies and kids again. I couldn't wait to get there and love on them.

The return flight, on the other hand, just got tougher. There was way too much time to think and reflect on all the horrific things that I had seen and experienced. Things that were now implanted on my heart and in my mind.

Much like my hot showers, I unknowingly came up with a way, right or wrong, to handle the long flights home. I took two over the counter sleeping pills, put in my earplugs, turned on my iPod and listened to Christian music. Then I would drift off to sleep. Sometimes I woke up just long enough to use the restroom, and when I did, I returned to my seat and went right back to sleep.

Rarely would I allow myself to think about the children, let alone think about the specifics that I might have encountered on each trip.

Now I know what you're thinking - this is a recipe for disaster, and you're right. But when you're in the thick of it all, you do what you need to survive. As unhealthy as it was, I rarely allowed myself to think or talk about what I experienced on my trips to the orphanage. When I did talk about it, it was almost always to my husband—no one else. It was just too hard to think or talk about the children.

It was also during those years that my relationship with God started to deepen. One of the core Bible verses used in orphan ministry and the adoption community is James 1:27. It reads "Religion that God our Father accepts as pure and faultless is this: to look after orphans and widows in their distress..."

I can remember asking God, of all the things You ask us to do, why did You choose to care for orphans and widows as what defines pure and faultless religion?

This is strictly my own thoughts, but I don't believe it's there to define religion, rather it describes who God is—He is love. Jesus told us that the two greatest commands are to love God and to love others (paraphrased Matt. 22:37,39).

By loving the children at the orphanage and serving their hearts and their physical needs, I was allowing God's love to flow through me. It wasn't me loving and serving; it was Him.

I was simply mirroring my Father by loving those precious children the same way He loves me (and the same way He loves you!) The more I loved and cared for them, the more I started to take on the Father's heart.

During those years, I grew closer to God, and my relationship with Him became more and more intimate. My time reading His Word was no longer just a part of my morning routine, rather it had come alive and breathed truth and wisdom into my heart no matter what I was going through or what I needed each day.

My prayers were no longer filled with "I want, and I need", rather they turned into prayers for others rather than for myself.

The Father's heart is for the orphan, and what He was teaching me during that time is that we are all orphans. We all walk through this life experiencing hurt, loss, grief, abandonment, rejection, abuse, and neglect. Most of all, we are all in need of a Father who loves us unconditionally. We all need a Father who gives us a home to live with Him forever. And that's exactly what He does, just as Jesus promised: "I will not leave you as orphans; I will come to you." (John 14:18)

During that time, God revealed to me so much more about who He really is. He showed me that while He is the all-powerful, omnipotent God of the Universe, He is also our loving Father who cares about every detail of our hearts and lives. While He wants you to be obedient to Him and while He wants you to serve Him, more than anything, His greatest desire for you is to spend time with Him in His presence. He is God, and He needs nothing from us other than our hearts of love.

I want to close this chapter by speaking to those of you who may be reading this while you are in the middle of a very dark season. As I shared earlier, I have suffered my own dark seasons, something I will share more about as we move further into this book.

Maybe what I've shared in this chapter is just too hard for you to hear right now and you either can't or won't accept it. You know what, that's okay. It's okay to read my words and shake your head thinking, "No, that's not true for me," as you read.

Give yourself permission to feel hurt and angry. You cannot undo what God has promised you. You cannot cause Him to love you any less. Even if you think otherwise, He will never stop loving you.

There is nothing you are thinking or feeling that He doesn't already know, so there is no need to try to hide it or deny it. Allow yourself to feel the hurt and grief that you are currently walking through and know that it's not the end. It will not always be this way.

Maybe you are at the beginning of your journey. Maybe you are in the middle of your journey. But no matter where you are in the journey, you are not at the end.

Your story is not over. Your journey is a process, and everyone's way of walking through their season of sorrow looks different.

Leave these words parked inside your heart as you continue to move through these pages. (Remember the promise you made to yourself—just keep going!)

Chapter 4
Lucy And Mary

It was time to make another trip to China to check on the kiddos and our programs. By this point, we were making 2-4 trips a year. On each trip, we spent a day or two with the babies and a few days with the preschoolers.

On this particular trip, some of the team arrived before me so I was not able to see them until we met up at the orphanage on my first morning in China. I was told that they were on the sixth floor with the preschoolers, so I made my way up to them on the elevator.

As soon as the elevator doors opened, I heard an older child wailing, "Maaa ma! Maaa ma!" I thought, "Who is that?!" One thing about our work with the children is that we never heard the word "mama" spoken in the orphanage. I ran to the accordion gate, and I started shaking it as hard as I could yelling, "Ayi! Ayi!" Out popped the ayi running down the hallway to let me inside.

Not far behind her was one of our board members, Susan. She looked frantic as she and the children started running toward the gate as well. All the while this little girl was following alongside Susan and crying, "Maaa ma."

The child was sobbing, and I did not recognize her as one of the children who lived there. She appeared to be between eight and ten years old. I frantically asked Susan, "What on earth is going on and who is this child?" With a hurt-filled voice Susan said, "Oh Vickie, she is just breaking my heart. She just arrived a few days ago and she will not stop crying and calling out for her mama."

The little girl whom we later named Lucy, was the most recent addition to the orphanage. She clearly had cognitive delays. One could only assume that her family could no longer provide the care she needed, and they abandoned her. Though it had been several days since she was abandoned, sweet Lucy was still crying for her mama.

Oh, my heart. I'm telling you; my mama's heart was right there with Susan's. I could hardly stand the pain that this child was enduring. I considered what if my own children were separated from me. What if it was them calling out my name? How would they feel if I could not get to them? My heart broke for little Lucy.

As our years working in the orphanage progressed, the types of children who arrived at the orphanage began to change. We were seeing fewer babies and instead we were seeing an influx of older children arriving at the orphanage. Additionally, we began to see an increase in the number of children who had special needs.

The babies who were abandoned not only had special needs, but their needs were significant. The days of simple heart conditions and cleft lip/cleft palates were no longer the norm. We began to receive more babies who had missing arms and legs, missing eyes, complex heart, and abdominal conditions, among many other significant medical issues.

As for the older children, we were receiving a mix - some children with special needs and others without. Poverty, an increase in crime and parents facing incarceration directly impacted the influx of older children who had no one to care for them.

All this combined, made our work even more difficult as we tried to adjust our programs and deepen our pockets to help the orphanage meet the growing needs of these children.

As for Lucy, she cried from the time we arrived until the time we left each day. We continued with our work as best we could despite her visible devastation. Lucy sat on the floor at the end of the hall, pressing her face against the accordion gate so that she had a clear view of both the elevator door and the stairway. Each day she sat there watching and waiting for her mama to come while crying and calling for her. Everyday. All. Day. Long.

We took turns visiting with Lucy, trying to coax her to come to the classroom and play with the other children. We gave her toys to try to entice her, and a few times we were successful in getting her to join us. But in the end, Lucy was not going to take any chances of missing her mama coming up those stairs or walking out of that elevator door.

On the last day of our trip, we were in the classroom with the kids. I could hear Lucy down the hall crying for her mama. My heart just couldn't take it anymore. I walked to where she was perched in her waiting spot, and I sat down on the floor beside her.

Now I knew she couldn't understand anything I said, but I had to say it anyway. I used my comforting mama voice and said, "Lucy, I am so sorry that you have lost your mama. I know how much you miss her, and I know that you are scared in this place. I am so, so sorry Lucy. I wish I could fix this for you. I would if I could, but I can't. If it's okay with you, can I sit here with you for a while and keep you company?" At that point, Lucy reached over and picked up my hand and put it on her leg. Then she proceeded to place her hand on top of mine and started to pat my hand as if she were comforting me.

That was all it took. I couldn't take the heartache anymore. There I was trying to comfort this little girl and in return, she was trying to comfort me. We both sat there on the floor unable to understand each other, and yet somehow in that moment, we understood each other's hearts perfectly.

That day I broke my number one rule, which was to never let the children or the staff see me cry.

I never wanted them to think that I felt sorry for them. I never wanted the children to misinterpret my tears and think that I disapproved of their lives. I never wanted the staff to think that I was disappointed with the way that they cared for the children. But in that moment, I physically could not hold back my tears.

Lucy and I sat there for the longest time, crying and comforting each other. We waited there together for her mama to come and rescue her.

LUCY HOLDING VICKIE'S HAND

What happens to the human heart, like Lucy's, when we are rejected and left by someone who no longer wants us?

How does one move forward in life recovering from that type of rejection and loneliness?

How do we reconcile being the innocent person who has done absolutely nothing to deserve what has been done to us? How do we forgive? How do we learn to trust and love again? And then there is the even bigger question, why did God allow this to happen to Lucy? Why did God allow this to happen to the other orphans? Why does God allow any of us to be abandoned by a loved one? These are just some of the questions that began to consume my heart and mind as I served these beautiful children.

MARY

One of our older kids at the orphanage was a girl who appeared to be about sixteen years old. She had the most beautiful smile. She had some type of special need, although I wasn't sure what it was. We were told that she had grown up in the orphanage, but no one was sure if she had arrived as a baby or as a preschooler. We decided to give her the name of Mary.

The way Mary walked and carried the left side of her body was like that of someone who had suffered a stroke. Her feet were sluggish, and she walked with a noticeable limp. Though she appeared to have all her fingers, they were all turned under so all you could see were her knuckles.

Mary loved to stand at the window outside in the hallway watching the children and our team play in the preschool classroom. You could tell that Mary looked forward to our visits as she would come running towards us when she saw us arrive. She always greeted us with her beautiful smile, and she would lock arms with one of us and escort us down the hall to the classroom.

During my visits, I always made sure to spend time with Mary, talking with her through a translator. We took her gifts of hair barrettes and bows to wear in her hair. She was such a pretty girl, inside and out, and we wanted her to know just how special she was to us.

MARY AND VICKIE

During one of our trips, a team member asked Mary what she would like to have as a gift. Mary requested slippers for her feet. We had no idea that the same condition that was causing her fingers to turn under was also impacting her toes.

The team member found a pair of slip-on shoes and using elastic string, we were able to make shoes for Mary that were much like ballerina slippers. When we placed them on her feet, we were overcome by the odor.

The smell was horrendous. We asked the nurse and pediatrician from our team if they would look at Mary's feet. When they examined her, it was discovered that parts of her toes and her fingers were slowly wasting away. It was as if her flesh was rotting, causing her to slowly lose her fingers and toes.

The picture of what happened that day will forever be etched in my mind. As Mary sat on a chair, and Susan sat beside her, the nurse and doctor knelt in front of Mary and washed her feet, trying to clean years' worth of build-up from under the crevices of her toes. Mary was visibly embarrassed and was concerned with how she would complete her daily chore of laundry if they placed the ointment on her hands.

NURSE BREAKING DOWN IN GRIEF

Standing in front of me was the re-creation of Jesus washing the disciple's feet. The smell of Mary's feet was so horrible, and the damage that had been done from years' worth of neglect was more than they could stand. The nurse finally stopped what she was doing. She was so overcome by grief that she broke down in tears. These were two women who had devoted their careers to caring for children with special needs, but to see a child in such condition from so many years of neglect was more than their hearts could handle.

They eventually were able to continue and was able to clean underneath all of Mary's fingers. They supplied her with her own washcloths and special soap so that she could keep herself clean.

Experiencing God in THE HIDDEN PLACE

Once we left the orphanage, we knew Mary would be on her own to maintain cleaning her fingers and toes.

When our team returned the next day, there greeting us at the gate was Mary and her beautiful smile. She was wearing her new shoes, and she had her hair all fixed up. She took turns calling each of us mama in the hopes that one of us would someday decide to take her home.

I have some beautiful pictures of our time spent with Mary. In every picture, she is always smiling. Nothing seemed to ever get her down.

The following year we hosted a summer camp for the preschoolers and teens from the orphanage. The day came for our preschoolers to have an outing. It would be the first time we took the preschoolers outside the gates of the orphanage.

We had a day packed full of fun activities, and we wanted to be sure Mary was invited to come along for the day.

We were meeting the kids at the local McDonald's. I'll never forget seeing Mary being helped down out of the bus. She was wearing a gorgeous baby blue cotton skirt with a white blouse. She wore a matching blue bow in her hair, and her smile that day was more beautiful than ever. She told us that it was the first time she had ever left the orphanage. Additionally, it was her very first time in a vehicle. At sixteen years old she was getting to experience everyday freedom we all take for granted. Can you imagine?

After lunch at McDonald's, we walked across the street to the local mall which had an indoor playhouse. You should have seen Mary's eyes light up. Because she couldn't handle all the walking, the orphanage had brought along a wheelchair. Mary told us through the translator that she always dreamed about what it would be like to go to a mall.

After the mall, we headed over to the beach. Mary was

able to see the ocean for the first time in her life. She sat on the sand and watched the waves roll in as the children played on the beach.

Throughout the day I looked to find Mary to see how she was doing. Every time I spotted her; she was absolutely beaming. For the first time in her life, she was able to experience life like a normal person. For the first time in her life, she was doing all the things a teenage girl her age should be doing.

What a precious blessing it was to be a part of Mary's special day.

After years of witnessing suffering and experiencing so much injustice, the questions I started to ask myself were as many as the number of children I watched suffer alone day after day. The children sat locked up within their own personal prisons of human suffering, and the trauma they endured was beyond comprehension.

For me, Lucy was the child who started to cause my heart to churn and question. At first, I couldn't understand why this little girl had impacted me differently than the other children. But the longer I thought about it I soon realized that while her abandonment was no greater or less than the other children in the orphanage, the impact of her abandonment was different because she had once known the love of a family - more specifically, the love of a mother.

She knew love. She knew compassion. She knew the difference between her home and the orphanage. She knew what it was like to have a mama bathe her. She knew about washing and styling her hair. Lucy knew that children didn't belong locked up in a big huge sterile building, having to shave their heads to prevent lice. She knew what it was like to be cared for and nurtured, and she knew that what she was now enduring in the orphanage was dramatically and traumatically different than life with a loving family. She belonged at home with her family, and she knew that.

It was after that trip that things began to shift in my heart. I was beginning to feel very unsettled and unsure about my future working in orphan ministry.

I went through a season of seeking God, trying to better understand our work and whether that was actually what He wanted for me. If there is one thing I have learned through the years of serving God is that when you are in the center of His will and doing what He calls you to do, your heart will experience peace.

Even when there are rough seasons and challenges in the work you are doing, He gives you His peace knowing that you are where you are meant to be, doing what you are called to do.

But it's when your heart starts getting wobbly that it's time to sit up and take notice. Clearly, my heart was starting to feel wobbly.

I spent months in prayer and in His word asking Him what He wanted me to do. Was He really calling me out of orphan ministry? There was still so much work to be done, but my heart was very unsettled.

Oh, I still loved the children more than anything. I loved them so much, and I loved spending time with them. But there was a dissatisfaction inside of my heart that I couldn't seem to shake or understand.

The programs seemed to no longer satisfy my desire to help the children. I never felt like I was doing enough for them. None of it ever felt like it was enough of what they needed. I knew in my heart, they needed families. Though I knew I couldn't control their circumstances, advocating for them through various adoption groups and social media outlets didn't seem like enough. I wanted more.

So, where did that leave me? What did the feeling that I was experiencing mean? Could it be that God was calling me out of the field of serving the fatherless? After months of praying about it, I finally decided I was going to take some time away to attend a weekend retreat for women. Despite it being a writer and speaker conference, I felt like I needed the time away by myself to seek God about all that was happening in my heart.

It was the last day of the conference, and I woke up early to make sure I had enough time to have my devotions before breakfast and our first session. I opened my Bible and happened to land on Isaiah 61.

It read, "The Spirit of the Sovereign Lord is on me, because the Lord has anointed me to proclaim good news to the poor. He has sent me to bind up the brokenhearted, to proclaim freedom for the captives and release from darkness for the prisoners." (Isaiah 61:1)

As soon as I read those verses, God spoke straight to my heart. He was not calling me out of the fields, rather He was asking me to go deeper. He was asking me to not only bind up the brokenhearted, but to also proclaim freedom to the children who were being held captive in the orphanage—to release them out of their darkness.

I went home that weekend with a clarity that I had never had before. The peace was so great, and I finally knew what He was asking me to do. Just like before, I had no idea how to get to where He was asking me to go, but what I knew was that He had led me before and he would lead me again. My role was to simply follow His lead—to just keep saying yes to Him.

Chapter 5
The Big Yes

When God placed me in China to serve orphans, He pulled back the curtain revealing to me many of the things which were hidden away inside the hearts of the children. Little by little, the orphanage would give us more and more access to floors of children, and little by little we gained a fuller understanding of their everyday realities.

When God pulled back that curtain, He allowed my eyes to see through His eyes. He allowed my heart to feel through His heart. He gave me a front-row seat to brokenness, grief, sorrow, abuse, and neglect, and I began to better understand what such trauma does to the human soul and mind.

He allowed me to see and feel so much of the hurt that His own heart carries and endures as He loves these orphans. This revealing expanded beyond the orphans, and I began to have a deeper understanding of the Father's love toward all of us here on this earth as we walk through the hurts, trials, and suffering that comes from living in a sin-filled world.

God knew these were things I would need to know to continue how He was calling me to serve.

It was at that conference that God opened my eyes and

The Big Yes

showed me what He wanted us to do next. We had already been serving in China for more than seven years at that point. After that weekend we started to have conversations with the orphanage about what God had revealed to me: foster care. Simultaneously, my husband and I started to pray about moving to China to run a foster care program that would serve the aging orphans.

Despite the relationship we had established with the orphanage directors and staff, asking them to hand over their children to be raised by foreigners was a whole different level of trust. At first, they refused, but we kept praying for God to change their hearts. Eventually, the orphanage conceded. They agreed to start by giving us two children. This was just one of many confirmations God gave us that it was time to take the next step in our yes.

After many months of prayer, we had such a peace. We knew without a doubt that God was calling us to move to China with our family to set up the foster program, and to provide care for these children.

We slowly began giving away all our things, with our home being the last thing to go. We knew that selling our home served as the final green light we needed to make the move. When it sold, we gave away the rest of our things including our vehicle, furniture, and clothing. It was time to leave.

I know this all sounds so quick and easy, but I can assure you it was a process. Between the time God revealed His plan to me at that conference and the time we boarded the plane for our move to China, two years had elapsed.

We spent those two years in constant prayer, seeking God's will for our lives. We had our children to consider - three adult children who were living on their own and four children still at home. In addition to the initial two children we adopted from China, we adopted two more by this point. We now had four children adopted from China. We were faced with moving them back to their birth country even though they were very much Americanized.

Then there was the issue of Jim's job. He had a wonderful job with the State of Ohio where he had worked for over twelve years. Not to mention, both Jim and I still had living parents. So many people would be impacted by our decision, and with heartfelt prayers, we considered each one of them.

Ultimately, we decided indeed to move to China. Was it an easy decision? Yes and no. It was easy to say yes to God because we trusted Him wholeheartedly. We trusted Him with our children, and we trusted Him in what He was calling us to do. We knew He would not do anything to hurt us nor our kids, and like I would always tell people, the safest place you can ever be is in the will of God.

The part that wasn't easy was leaving behind our adult children, our families, and our church community. That was the hardest part. We were close to our children and families. To know we were walking away from being with our parents during the last season of their lives made our choice very difficult.

When it came time to leave, each of us had one suitcase filled with our respective clothing and personal items. The kids were able to take a few of their Legos, their handheld games and DVDs. The rest of the things we needed to set up our home, we purchased once we arrived in China.

The first two months in China were spent setting up our home and adjusting to our new lives. We were learning to establish new routines that came with living in a third world country.

Since there were six of us, we used the public bus for transportation. This was a first for us. We lived very close to the south equator, almost directly on the South China Sea. Saying it was hot and tropical was an understatement, as the heat index averaged 120 degrees in the summer.

We were eventually able to secure a home to rent for the foster home that was located just two doors down from our home.

God's provisions were overflowing. Everything was easy, yet nothing was easy. We always had exactly what we needed when we needed it, but our adjustments to shopping, cooking and everyday living was hard.

The day finally arrived for us to travel to the orphanage to bring our first two babies to the foster home. We were so excited. The goal of our foster home was to provide a family environment for children who were medically stable yet struggling to adjust to the orphanage environment. The end goal was to help these children to catch up developmentally and ultimately advocate for their adoption.

We were at the orphanage and had our first two babies ready to go when an ayi came walking down the hall with a tiny baby in her arms. The baby could not have weighed more than nine or ten pounds, even though she was at least twelve months old. The ayi said that the baby had problems eating and she really needed our help. Well, the answer was yes, of course! We'd take her! So instead of going home with two babies that day, we went home with three.

That first day set the tone for what was ahead of us. It was the first of many miracles we would witness. For so long we were told no, we could not establish a foster program. Then we were told we could only have two babies. Then we went home with three babies. And within nine months of opening the foster home, we had twelve babies and a long list of more babies waiting to enter our home.

God flooded our ministry with His favor and provisions.

Experiencing God in THE HIDDEN PLACE

We had unexpected monetary donations, a local vendor provided us bread and meat daily, and we had people knock on our door to give us gifts and food for the children.

Local organizations provided us with diapers and formula. We saw children physically and miraculously healed. We had volunteers come from America to help us care for the children. We received recognition from the local newspaper for our work, and local government officials visited our home, bringing us donations of food and supplies and thanking us for taking care of their children.

The best part of all was the exposure our children received through word of mouth in the adoption community and social media. The before and after pictures of their transformations were astounding.

ORIGINAL SIX FOSTER CHILDREN

There was absolutely no magic formula for what we were doing. It was as simple as providing our children with a home filled with love. We gave them the nutrition they needed to physically recover and grow, while simultaneously giving them a safe and loving environment to heal from their wounds of trauma and neglect.

For the first time in their lives, they were learning how to be children and what being loved felt like.

Chapter 6

Mimi

Our children were being adopted and given the gift of a forever family, which meant we had space to bring even more children home to us.

Early on we assessed the capacity of the ministry to understand what resources we had. With the staff that we hired; we knew that we had enough resources to accept a few more babies to the home. I called our friend at the orphanage and told her that we hoped to add two more babies to the program. I asked if we could visit the orphanage to begin the selection process.

Of the selection process, people often asked me, "How on earth did you choose which babies when there are so many in need?" My answer was always, "we didn't choose." Jim and I approached the selection process by separately going through the rows of cribs while praying and asking for the Holy Spirit to guide us. As the Holy Spirit would press upon our hearts different children, we prayed and asked God questions about the child. We spent time watching to see how the baby was developing, and most importantly we paid close attention to the baby's emotional state.

As I shared earlier, the goal of our ministry was to bring children to our foster home who were medically stable but were unable to cope emotionally with the daily trauma of the abuse and neglect they experienced in the orphanage. Many children develop coping mechanisms to survive, however, many do not. Right or wrong, the babies we most desired to help were those who did not have the coping mechanisms to adequately survive the orphanage environment.

On this visit, there was a baby in the very back of the row who was sitting upright and staring straight ahead at seemingly nothing. She didn't have any facial expressions. She just sat there lifeless. We were told that she was twenty months old, and despite her age, she was extremely tiny. I asked the staff a few questions about her, and they said that she was a good baby. She never cried, and she didn't have much of an appetite. While this may seem like an unusual definition of a "good baby," in an orphanage setting with dozens and even hundreds of babies, the quiet and low maintenance children are labeled as "good."

I jotted down the baby's name and her birthdate and moved on.

After every visit, Jim and I spent time intentionally praying about the orphanage visit, asking God to guide us in our decision to select the next child(ren) to our foster home. Jim and I prayed together and then we prayed separately. We would then come back together and talk about our visit. We went over our notes about which babies we felt that God was drawing us towards, and without fail there was always one or two babies who appeared on both of our lists.

This particular visit was different because while the baby in the back row made both our lists, she didn't fit the criteria we had established for our ministry. And yet clearly the Holy Spirit had highlighted her to both of us. I remember the conversation so vividly. Jim and I were both concerned about this baby's future. Our program was designed to help those who were medically stable, giving the babies the extra attention, they needed to better their chances of one day being adopted. It was not our intention to create a home that provided long term housing and care for children. A child with elevated medical needs would demand more than we could provide, and such demands would be a disservice to the hope of placing the child into a forever family.

I can remember telling Jim that this baby needed so much more than we could ever offer her. She needed physical therapy, occupational therapy, speech therapy—you name it and I was sure that she would need it. Even then, we had no idea what her actual needs were. The orphanage staff said that her adoption file indicated that she had developmental delays. I raised my eyebrow when they told me this because from what I could see of the child, there was no way to actually know what was going on with her.

One of the hardest things about a child who has come from a place of abuse and neglect, such as an orphanage setting, is trying to decipher if it is an actual special need the child was born with or a result of the environment they came from. Then there are times when the child does have a special need, but the abuse and neglect have magnified and exacerbated it to a level much worse than it would be otherwise.

With this baby, the unknowns were many. Jim and I both kept coming back around to the same conclusion that we simply did not have the resources to provide what this child needed.

We decided to go back to the orphanage and take another walkthrough of the nursery. For the first time, we wavered with our decision. We absolutely did not believe that we had the resources to give this baby the help she needed and yet neither of us could shake what felt like the Holy Spirit's prompting for us to consider this child for our program.

We knew that if we took her, we were probably looking at long term care, which meant we would lose an opening for a child in the future who we were better able to help. But we could also see that this little girl was worsening before our very eyes. Her face was starting to carry a permanent dazed expression, and she just sat there lifeless. She was exhibiting many obvious signs of a child diagnosed with "failure to thrive."

Later that afternoon I received an email from an adoption agency from the States. They said that one of their families had accepted a referral of a baby who lived in the orphanage with which we were partnering. They gave me the baby's name and birthdate. The agency wanted to know if I knew of the child and whether I could share anything about her.

When I saw the name of the baby my heart sunk. I was pretty sure it was the same baby Jim and I had been struggling with whether to bring home. I quickly grabbed my notebook to look through the names of the babies and there it was. My scribbled note beside this baby's name read, "Nobody is home?"

I called for Jim to come upstairs. When he arrived, I read him the email. I looked up from my computer and said, "I don't know about you, but I think this is a game-changer." He said, "Absolutely it's a game-changer. We've got to bring that baby home, or she won't even make it to her adoption day."

There was this huge sense of urgency that came over my heart. I needed to get to that baby as quickly as possible. I called the orphanage to have them get her ready because we were heading over.

When we walked into the nursery, they were finishing

putting a diaper and clothes on her. I'll never forget them placing her in my arms. The staff worker reminded me, "Don't forget, she doesn't like to eat."

She was as light as a feather, and her little body felt like a rag doll in my arms. She was so soft, and she felt so squishy; she had very low muscle tone. She showed no response to me holding her. She didn't look at me. She simply dropped her head and it laid like a dead weight on my shoulder.

One of our board members had messaged me earlier and said that she wanted to name this new baby Mimi in honor of her grandmother who was her hero for being such a brave and strong woman. So, we did; we named the baby "Mimi."

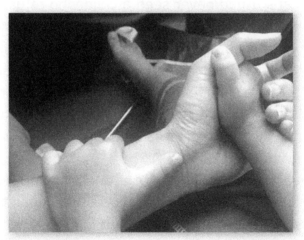

THE RIDE HOME—MIMI HOLDING VICKIE'S HAND

When we arrived home, I quickly undressed Mimi to put fresh clothes on her. What I saw will forever be etched into my mind. The many layers of clothing that she had been wearing concealed just how small Mimi really was. Her ribs were showing, and my fingers overlapped when I put them around her tiny arm.

Mimi was twenty months old and weighed about fifteen pounds. The tears started to flow as my mind began to process the reality of what I was seeing. By this point, I had been working in this orphanage for many years, and I had seen lots and lots of underweight and malnourished babies. The seeping from their eyes and frailty of their bodies was nothing new to me. Yet Mimi's condition seemed worse than any baby I had met before.

I had learned very quickly that no matter how old a child was when I picked them up, I would always put a hand behind the baby's head like one would with a newborn baby. I never knew if the baby had the strength to hold up his or her head or not.

But this was very different. In all my years of working with orphans, I had never seen a child who refused to eat. It was as if she literally was willing herself to die.

I asked myself, "How bad does it have to get for a twenty-month-old baby to choose death? How bad does it have to get for a child to decide, 'You know what, this is just too hard. I can't do this anymore. I'm checking out.' What type of horrific things had happened to this child to bring her to that moment?"

My heart was absolutely torn, and I could feel the hot tears rolling down my face as I picked her up and held her as tightly as I could. I whispered out loud, "Father, help me to help this baby."

I went to the kitchen and made her a warm bottle. As soon as she saw it, she started screaming. The fear in her face said it all. They had clearly been trying to force-feed her. I tried to feed her with a spoon instead. That was even worse.

She immediately put her thumb in her mouth and blocked anything I attempted to feed her. I started praying - begging

God to give me wisdom in what to do. I finally decided I would try an eyedropper. I filled the eyedropper with a mixture of warm milk and cereal, and I slipped it into the corner of her mouth. Slowly I squeezed. I caressed her cheek and throat while talking gently to her. "Come on baby girl. You can do this. You are safe now. I love you and I will take care of you. I will never let anyone hurt you ever again."

Even though I knew she didn't understand a word that I was saying, she began to swallow small amounts of the milk and cereal mixture. She literally groaned in displeasure because she absolutely did not want to eat. This went on for about an hour and then she finally had enough. She refused to take any more. My heart sunk when I looked at the bottle to see that in all my effort, she had only consumed a fraction of what her malnourished body needed.

She was exhausted and so was I. It was bedtime, so I made the decision that I would put her to bed for the evening and try again the next morning. For the first time in my life, I put a child to bed who I knew had an empty stomach, and it tore my heart to shreds.

I cried all the way back to our house. Jim knew when I walked in the door that I had been unsuccessful in adequately feeding Mimi. I cried in his arms as I poured out my heart to him. I had never seen a child so broken and so wounded.

That night I sent an email to our prayer team and asked for intercessory prayer. I shared the reality of what we were dealing with and told them that I had no idea how I was going to help this baby. I needed wisdom. I not only needed wisdom, but I needed a feeding specialist. I knew I was in way over my head and I had no idea what to do to help her.

I shut down my laptop, took a hot shower and went to bed. I woke up early the next morning and went down to the baby house. I told the staff that it was crucial that only I fed and cared for Mimi—no one else.

The staff was confused, but I knew in my heart that if this baby was going to live, she needed to eat. And the only way that Mimi would eat was if she learned to trust me. I went to her crib and found her there wide awake. I greeted her with a smile, and I gave her a big wet kiss on her cheek. I held her tightly as I told her how much I loved her. Then I began the process of feeding her just like I had done the night before.

Little by little she took more and more food from the dropper. I fed that child like a little bird for days. Though she remained limp and lifeless in my arms, showing no emotions and making zero eye contact with me, slowly but surely, she was eating!

While the food was keeping her alive physically, the reality was I still had no idea how to reach the soul of this child. She was so broken. When I looked into her eyes, it was as if they were transparent and I could see right through them. I cried out to God for help. "Father, please help me. I don't know what to do to help this baby. I don't know what I'm doing. I don't know how to reach her!"

During naptime a few days later, I was getting ready to shut down my laptop when a message popped up from a sweet friend of mine on our prayer team in the States.

The message read, "Hey guys, 1:48 am here and woke up praying with you all on my mind. Heard the word "sing". Sing to Mimi. Praying for wisdom and insight, peace and love. Thank you for being His arms and feet here on this earth. Love you all, Kim."

I read it and then said out loud, "Sing! I can do that! I can sing!" Then I thought, "But what? What should I sing?" Immediately 'Jesus Loves Me' came to my mind.

I shut down my computer and ran to the house. I reached down and picked up Mimi from her crib. I plopped down in the rocking chair in the nursery, and I held her. As usual, she dropped her head and laid it on my shoulder.

I started to sing Jesus Loves Me, and before I got to the words "the Bible" she popped her head up off my shoulder and looked me square in the eye. I was stunned. She made direct eye contact with me for the first time!

I said, "Oh you like that do you?" She put her head back on my shoulder and I continued to sing. Within seconds I could feel her little body relaxing as she physically seemed to be cuddling up against me instead of just laying on me.

This was the assurance that I needed. Indeed, someone was at home inside of Mimi. Locked deep down inside of all the brokenness there was a little girl who was most certainly alive.

From that moment on, I rocked her, and I sang. Again, and again and again. I cannot tell you the number of times I sang that song to her. I tried other children's songs, but the only song she responded to was 'Jesus Loves Me.' So, Jesus Loves Me I sang!

I was so excited at what I thought was a breakthrough. Mimi clearly enjoyed the song, and she continued to eat for me, but there still were no other signs of life coming from this sweet little broken child.

It was a Sunday afternoon and our staff had the day off, so our family was working at the house. Rather than putting Mimi down for a nap, I decided to hold her and rock her while she napped. I was praying over her, and I can remember feeling so helpless and discouraged.

I knew I wasn't enough. I was so overwhelmed by her needs, and I knew in my humanness that I had absolutely nothing to offer her.

In my hands, I held the most broken child I had ever known. She was broken physically, emotionally and even spiritually - her soul had been stolen by the abuse and neglect. I cried out to God once again, "Father, I don't know how to help this baby! I don't know what to do! How can I fix her? I need wisdom! Show me how to love her!"

It was in that moment that He whispered to my heart, "Look beyond the brokenness and see the beauty in her that I see."

I was so surprised. It sounded so simple. Little did I know what was about to happen next, would forever change my life.

Suddenly, as I sat there rocking Mimi, it felt as if someone was pouring warm oil over my head. I squeezed Mimi tighter as I felt the oil flow over my head and down over my body. I felt it moving down my arms and through my fingertips.

Instantly I started crying; actually, I was sobbing. I had this overwhelming sense of warmth, peace, and love. Oh, there was so much love that was invading every inch of my being. It felt as if the love had completely overtaken me. I was crying so hard that I could hardly breathe.

I sat there very still as I realized that I was experiencing the physical love of God flowing through my body, and that His love was being poured into the little broken body that I was holding in my arms.

I knew without a shadow of a doubt that God was touching this baby with His healing and love.

From that moment on, everything changed. While every day was still a struggle for her, I knew she had been touched by His Healing Hand. What was even crazier was that I had been touched as well.

The love that He poured over me never left. Every time I

held Mimi the tears started flowing with an overwhelming sense of love for her. I held her and rocked her for hours.

I would tell Jim over and over again, "I love this baby so much. She is so beautiful. I can hardly stand it. I just love her so much." It became a joke because every time I held her; I went into the same speech. Then one day Jim said, "I know, I know...you love Mimi so much. I get it!" We both laughed, but honestly, I couldn't help myself. God filled me with His love for her. When I talked to her, I cried. When I looked at her, I cried. Even the thought of tiny Mimi filled me instantly with God's oozing love, and I cried.

Every day brought more and more healing to Mimi. This healing eventually turned into smiles and then ultimately giggles. His Love. His Peace. His Joy resided in her. I would sneak up to the door of the playroom and stand watching her play with her toys. Life had entered back into her body and she was consumed with His joy. Many times, I would catch her smiling for what seemed like no reason at all. The power of God's miraculous love was so evident in Mimi.

Before my very eyes, I watched God bring her from brokenness to wholeness. My heart would swell with pride for her. I was so proud of her for not giving up on life. I was so proud of her for opening her heart just enough to let me in, no matter how small of an opening that was. I was completely undone by all the lessons that she had taught this ole gal's mama heart.

Soon Mimi and I became inseparable. When I walked into the room and Mimi saw me, she came crawling straight toward me. If she heard my voice, she turned to look for me. If I walked around the house doing chores, she followed me.

Experiencing God in THE HIDDEN PLACE

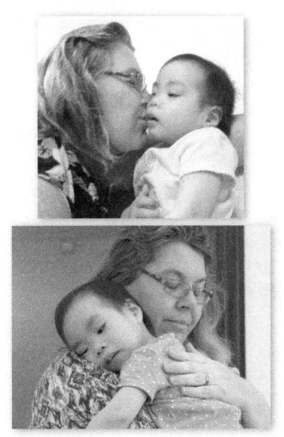

VICKIE HOLDING MIMI

Through this desperately broken little girl, I was given a front-row seat to experiencing God and His crazy, wild love for us. It was through this experience that He gave me a better understanding of how He feels as the Father to each of us. He is the giver of love, healing, joy, and peace to His children

I, for whatever reason, was given the privilege of experiencing just a taste of what He experiences when He looks at each of us. I was experiencing the magnificent love that swells up inside of Him as our Father. Through His eyes, you are His beautiful creation, and no matter what you have done, or how broken your life may be, His love

Mimi

for you cannot be undone. All that He sees is His beautiful righteous child.

The day finally arrived for Mimi to be adopted by her forever family. It was only a few days shy of two months since I first met Mimi. Honestly, it was one of the hardest things I ever had to do, and yet it was also one of the best days of my life as I placed Mimi into the loving arms of her forever mama.

What I didn't know then was that God was going to continue to use Mimi in my life in profound and beautiful ways. It began with the foundation that He laid on my heart, showing me what His love looks like for you and me.

Mimi was an abandoned baby on the other side of the world sitting in the back row of an orphanage, and God saw her. He not only saw her physically, but He heard her cries and knew her needs. From the world's perspective, this one little child was hidden away - lost and forgotten. But not to the God of the Universe. He sent someone to rescue her and bring her to Him so that He could heal her and make her whole again.

That would be the foundation that God would use for me in the days and months to come. He would use it to build the many lessons that my heart would soon learn. Little did I know that very soon, God was going to use Mimi to save me in my own season of sorrow and brokenness.

Chapter 7
He Gives And Takes Away

It was incredible to be a part of a ministry filled with God's grace, and the most important thing was it had nothing to do with us or our efforts. It was all God. He provided the hearts of cooperation with the Chinese government. He provided the home and the financial means, the help we needed with staff, and the volunteers to care for the children.

But as with every situation, there are two sides to the story. The day to day stress of running the ministry was daunting. We were running so hard to keep the daily operations going. Whether it was dealing with staff, negotiating supply prices, or dealing with the language barrier, it was hard work and we were physically and emotionally exhausted.

For the first nine months of the foster program, we did not have a Chinese manager who could speak with the staff or help us in our day to day business dealings. It was so hard. You can bet Google Translator became my best friend very quickly.

When I looked behind the curtain beyond of the daily progress of our children, the impact of trauma, abuse, and neglect were evident. It was such a difficult process to both physically care for our many children while also trying to tend to each child's unique emotional needs.

We were so thankful for all the experiences we had from adopting four of our own children from China, as well as working with the babies in the orphanage. Because we had witnessed so many children at the orphanage suffer, and because we had witnessed the realities of their daily lives, we had a front-row seat into the hearts of the children coming to us.

We know that if God had not given us those opportunities beforehand, we would have never been equipped to handle what our babies needed when they came home to us in the foster program. Nonetheless, the weight of all that was being absorbed into our hearts and minds, was taking a toll on us.

Jim and I regularly visited the orphanage each week. If we were not checking on the babies and our programs inside, we were taking one of our little ones for medical attention such as well checks and immunizations.

We were friends with all the staff, and we loved every minute of working with these people. We had developed such a wonderful relationship with the staff. We experienced mutual respect and honor, and it was a complete miracle that had God's fingerprints all over it.

As Jim and I would continue our visits to the orphanage, a new pattern started to emerge. We were beginning to see babies that were born with Down syndrome being abandoned. In all our years of serving we had only seen one other child with DS. The numbers of children with DS continued to grow, and God once again started to stir in our hearts a burden to help this population of children.

After praying and seeking God about how we could help, we felt He was leading us to open a second foster home just for children with Down syndrome. Within a few short months, God once again swung open the doors of cooperation and provisions.

We had a home made available to us right beside our first foster home. Additionally, we quickly received the financial provisions to renovate the home, fully equip it, and operate it for an entire year.

On the Fourth of July that year, we brought home every single baby in the orphanage with Down syndrome—not a single child was left behind. We were told that it was the largest exodus of children with Down syndrome from a single orphanage in the entire country of China. Only God!

CHILDREN, STAFF, AND VOLUNTEERS[1]

One day Jim and I headed to the orphanage for our weekly visit. As soon as we entered the baby nursery an ayi approached me, pulling my arm so that she could show me something. She brought me into the room that we called the "holding room." The holding room was in the front of the nursery, and the ayis used this room for babies who were sick and needed quarantined. They also used the holding room for new arrivals. Any child who needed to be assessed

He Gives And Takes Away

by a doctor because they were new or sick, was placed in the holding room until the orphanage doctor had time to assess or treat them.

The ayi led me to a crib on the far end of the room. She pointed down into the crib. There in front of me was a beautiful tiny baby, probably no more than a month old. I guessed her to weigh about seven or eight pounds, and I kind of chuckled because she had "chicken hair." Chicken hair is what we lovingly called a baby's hair if it stood straight up on the baby's head.

It was evident that this was a baby born with Down syndrome. I picked her up so carefully. She was so, so tiny. It had been so long since I had such a tiny baby in my arms. She was stunning! The thing I remember the most was that she immediately locked eyes with mine. She was so bright-eyed and so alert for such a young baby. I cuddled her close to my chest as I started to sway back and forth. I was absolutely in love with this little one.

Our friend and orphanage staff member came over and said, "Vickie, I'm sorry, but the doctors think this baby has a very sick heart." I told her that I'd like to have the baby sent to the hospital to have tests run. I assured her that we would pay for the tests. Arrangements were made for the baby to be sent to the hospital for testing, and several days later my friend called to inform me that the test results had returned. She said that we should come back to the orphanage to discuss the results with the doctors.

As soon as we arrived at the orphanage nursery, I went straight over to the baby's crib and picked her up. There was something very special about this baby, and I was drawn to her. I told Jim on the way over to the orphanage that I believed we were supposed to take her home with us. Jim said he had been feeling the same way.

Experiencing God in THE HIDDEN PLACE

When the doctor finally arrived, I could tell from the serious expression on his face that the results from the tests were not good. He proceeded to explain the results of her heart tests, and our manager translated it for us. The baby's condition was serious, and she would need open-heart surgery. While the orphanage could apply for funding to pay for this surgery, she was too young and too small to survive the surgery. But without it, she would die.

I told them, "Well her only chance is for us to take her home and pray she will grow big enough and strong enough to get the surgery she needs." Our manager gave her the name of Isabella and we brought little Isabella home to be a part of our foster family. We had to order a special formula that was higher in nutrition to help her grow. We had to get her newborn size diapers because she was so tiny.

Every day, several times a day, I went to the baby house and held Isabella. I was so drawn to her. I loved cuddling her and feeding her a bottle. She always looked up at me, locking her eyes with mine. I would take her upstairs to our prayer room and put on worship music. I would sit in the rocking chair and rock away as I prayed over her tiny body, contending for her healing, her growth, and her strength.

Early one morning, my phone rang. It was one of our volunteers. She said something was wrong with Isabella and I needed to come quick. I ran down to the house praying for God to give me His wisdom. As soon as I saw Isabella, I knew that she was in trouble. There was little color in her face; she was almost a pale grey.

I went to the medical closet and pulled out the oxygen reader and hooked it up to her little toe. As the numbers appeared, my heart sank as they started to slow down and eventually came to a stop. Her oxygen level should have been one hundred but instead, it was in the upper sixties.

Our sweet Isabella was in trouble. I pulled out my phone and called my friend at the orphanage, and I told her what was happening. I told her to call the doctor and get a bed ready; we were bringing Isabella right over.

I left the oxygen reader connected to her so that I could keep an eye on her levels. During the drive to the orphanage, I held her tight praying all the way there. "Father, please do not take this baby from me!"

The doctors were waiting for us, and as soon as I placed her in the crib, I stepped back to watch them work on her. They hooked her up to oxygen, and within a few short minutes, the numbers on the meter started to click up and the color began to return to her face. I could feel the relief as Jim and I stood there holding each other watching our sweet Isabella fight for her life.

That day we stayed with Isabella at the orphanage so that we could feed her and take care of her. The doctors kept telling us that we could go home, but there was no way I was going to leave my baby in that orphanage after everything she had been through. As the sun started to go down, my friend from the orphanage told me we needed to leave. They would not allow us to spend the night there, and Isabella would have to stay until she was stable enough to go home.

That was one of the longest rides home. I was physically sick to my stomach driving back home without Isabella in my arms. The worry of not being with her and not knowing how she was doing, weighed so heavy on my heart.

My friend called me several times a day to give me updates on Isabella. The doctors recommended she stay at the orphanage and get rest while they continued to monitor her condition. It was absolute agony not being with her. For several days I received updates. Following Isabella's condition was like riding a roller coaster—her progress was so up and down. We had our prayer team praying around the clock for her.

ISABELLA LOOKING AT VICKIE

About a week later, I received the dreaded phone call. Our Isabella had a massive heart attack. She did not survive. I could hear my friend telling me over and over again how sorry she was, but I was unable to speak. I just sat there and cried. She finally said that she was going to go ahead and hang up the phone. The only word I managed to form was, "Okay."

How does a mama's heart process the loss of a child? It is a feeling of sorrow like none other. While my heart knew she was no longer suffering, the depth of her loss was unbearable. Going into her room for the first time physically took my breath away. We had to pack away her little clothes and belongings in order to make room for another child. While the physical evidence of her life was gone, I carried our sweet Isabella in the deepest depths of my soul. My heart was devastated and filled with so much grief.

He Gives And Takes Away

I believe there are some very precious gems that God has placed in His Word for us. Gems that give us a glimpse of some of the very tender places of God's heart. When we lost Isabella my mind went to the very hard scene of Mary at the foot of the cross of Jesus. Despite Jesus having just been brutally beaten and nailed to a cross, He was moved with such compassion for His mother, Mary.

There Jesus hung in excruciating pain and suffering, yet His mind was on His mama who He knew was just a few short hours away of being asked to bury her own child. Jesus was moved with such deep compassion for what she was enduring, that He wanted to be sure that His mother would be taken care of once He was gone. (John 19:25-27).

The loss of Isabella was so hard on my heart, yet there was a comfort that came over my spirit as I recalled this precious gem recorded in God's word. The reality that came from the death of Isabella was yes, God had given us so much, and yes, He had also taken away

As we continued to move forward after Isabella's passing, the ministry God had built continued to drip in His favor. There was not a single request we put before Him that He would not only grant but grant extravagantly. There was nothing we needed that He did not provide. We were tired, but boy we were incredibly blessed! We loved serving the children and the ministry to which God had called us to.

Our testimony gave such faith and encouragement to so many people around the world who heard our story. From the very beginning, the only thing we wanted was to be obedient to whatever God called us to do. We trusted Him with our children and our lives, and we knew that as long as we did what He asked, everything would be okay. Or so we thought.

Chapter 8
The Horrible Day

In 2017 China released a new law pertaining to those foreign charities working in their country. As I began to read through the details, my heart sank. Even though our organization was an approved non-profit charity in the US, China now required all foreign organizations to apply, and be approved, as a non-profit charity in China.

The process was complex at best. Even though our organization had operated in China for over a decade, two years of which included operating our foster homes, we were now faced with the task of establishing ourselves as a non-profit charity in China. We worked hard over the next few months to gather the documentation needed to submit our registration. Our Chinese manager and I made our first trip to the provincial office to file our papers, knowing we were one of the first organizations in the country to apply under this new law.

One of the questions on the application asked for a description of the type of work we were doing. We listed all our programs; our summer teen camps and of course our foster care ministry. When the officer started to review our papers, he began asking our manager a lot of questions. Since they were speaking in Chinese, I had no idea what

The Horrible Day

they were saying, but I could tell from our manager's body language that she was getting nervous.

When they were finished, our manager turned and looked at me and said, "Vickie, he says that foster care is illegal in China and we need to send our babies back to the orphanage. Once we do that, we will be in compliance with the law, and then he will approve our application with no problem."

I sat there in shock. What did he mean foster care is illegal in China? That's ridiculous as everyone knew there were hundreds of foreign organizations in China providing foster care to orphans. And send our babies back to the orphanage? That was not an option. I told her to start negotiating and see what type of concessions they were willing to make. She did, and there were none. We left the office defeated. The moment I arrived home, I sent an SOS email to our prayer team.

Our prayer team, including our board members, was the heart of our ministry. We stayed completely transparent with them. We made sure that they always knew what was happening on the China side so that they knew exactly how to pray for the ministry and our needs.

Responses from our prayer partners started to flood my inbox as the team stormed the gates of heaven. We put out pleas via social media as well. There were hundreds of prayer warriors petitioning God to intervene and to once again change the hearts of the government officials like He had done so many times before.

No one doubted that God would hear and answer our prayers. We spent months praying and often fasting.

I cried out to God to please save our children. I knew it was not His will that they return to the orphanage. I knew it was not His will that they would be given to us to love only to be returned to a life of prison. I knew that He had called us to this ministry, and He had given us every single one of those children. I knew that He would turn this impossible situation around.

I had so much faith as I sat listening to the song, "Do It Again" by Elevation Worship. I played the song over and over. "I've seen you move the mountains, and I believe I'll see you do it again" was the line that I sang as I poured out my heart to God begging Him to please save our children.

During those months we made multiple trips to the provincial office trying to negotiate a way to keep our children. On our final trip to the provincial office, the officer told us there was no way around the situation. We had to return the children to the orphanage or face the consequences. When I told him that we were their family, his response was cold and abrupt. "They'll adjust," he said.

I can remember the flight home from that trip. It was the last flight of the night and everyone was resting with their overhead lights turned off. My manager and I sat quietly in shock, not saying a word.

I remember praying to God, "Surely this is not your will. We have done everything the law required us to do. We have operated completely ethically. We have been honest and forthright, not hiding anything. God, how can you let this happen to these innocent children?"

As I sat there praying with my eyes closed, there was a bump of turbulence, and I opened my eyes. I saw a Chinese man a few seats ahead of me on the other side of the aisle. His light was on and he was reading a Chinese newspaper.

I looked at the paper and blinked my eyes a few times trying to focus on what I was seeing. There on this Chinese newspaper was a picture of an American street sign written in English. The sign was from an intersection and the top

The Horrible Day

sign read, "Lies Street". The intersecting sign below it read, "Truth Avenue." And under Truth Avenue, another sign read, "One Way" with an arrow pointing in the same direction as Truth Avenue.

You can call this a coincidence if you'd like, but for me, it was God sending me a message. He was reminding me that in the midst of all that was happening, He was right there with me. He had a very clear message He wanted me to hear from Him.

I watched as the man folded up the paper and put it in the seatback in front of him. When we were unloading from the plane, he left the newspaper in the seatback pocket. As I walked by, I picked up the newspaper to keep.

God's message to me that night was very clear. There was only one way to travel through this process and that was along Truth Avenue.

I knew in my heart that we had told the truth and honored the laws of the Chinese government. As a result, we were going to lose all our children.

The next day I contacted the orphanage and set up a few meetings with the local officials. Many of those locals were our friends whom we had done business with for over a decade. We ate meals together. Our children played together. We visited each other's homes. But on that day, none of that seemed to matter.

For the first time since doing business in China, I witnessed the power that a communist country has on its people and its government officials. These officials—our friends for the past decade—were clearly afraid. They held in their hands an executive order from the higher-level provincial officials that said we were to return all the children to the orphanage.

I'll never forget the Director looking at me and asking,

Experiencing God in THE HIDDEN PLACE

"Will you comply with the law and return the children to our care?" I told her, "We did not come here to break your laws. Our intentions are the same today as they were when we came here ten years ago, and that is to help you however we can to care for the children in your care." She had a very sad and nervous look on her face, and with her eyes looking down, she said, "Thank you."

We discussed the details of returning the children and decided we would make the transition in about a week. We needed to talk to our staff and give them, and ourselves, as much time as possible to prepare our hearts to say goodbye to our kids.

I sobbed in Jim's arms all the way back home. I asked him, "Why is God not answering our prayers? Why is He allowing this to happen? Why would He let those people take our children? Why? Why? Why?" Jim didn't say a word; he just held me and let me lament.

My first telephone call was to our board members. This group of ladies had been in the thick of this journey alongside me every step of the way. Each of them had adopted from our orphanage. Each of them had been deeply invested in all the lives of the children from our orphanage.

I will never forget listening to them sob through the other end of the phone. Physically we were on opposite sides of the globe, but emotionally we were together as one. We are a tight-knit group of sisters in Christ, fellow mamas and fellow warriors who have served together through all the highs and lows that come with doing business in a communist orphanage.

Even though our family was physically on the front lines, these sisters were fighting mightily alongside us. Their love for the children was fierce and remains fierce even to this day.

The Horrible Day

After I spoke to our board, we met with our US volunteers who were living in China with us. These volunteers played a huge part in the daily lives of our children. Next came the dreaded conversation with our local staff - the babies' ayis. These ladies loved their babies something fierce, and when we shared the horrible news, their tears and wailing began immediately.

The ayis knew there was a new policy in place, but like us, they also knew we had a wonderful relationship with the government, the orphanage, and the police. They were just as shocked as we were. Their grief was almost unbearable to watch as once again, the reality of their lives living in a communist country was rearing its ugly head.

No matter the injustice and no matter their opinions, they never had any say over the decisions that their government made for their lives.

The nights were long, and there are no words to describe how our hearts ached. I kept waiting for God to turn everything around. I kept waiting for Him to swoop in and make things right just like He had always done before. But He didn't.

It was a Tuesday morning, just three days after our meeting with the local officials, and my cell phone rang. It was my friend from the orphanage whom I had worked with for the past decade. Despite her being a government employee, she was truly a friend to our family. She loved working at the orphanage, and she was such a blessing to us.

When I answered, her voice was panicked and filled with fear. She said, "Vickie, we have to come and get the children right now. Our director received a call last night at 10 pm from the provincial officials saying all children in the province who are in foster care have to be returned to the orphanage by 10:30 am the next morning." I looked at the clock. It was 9:30 am. She said they would be there in fifteen minutes. Then she said, "And Vickie," she paused for a moment, "The police may be coming as well. I'm so sorry. You have fifteen minutes to get the babies ready to go and we will be there."

I hung up the phone and sprang into action. The first thing I did was send a text to our adult daughter in America. I told her the police were coming to take all our babies. I told her to contact our church and get the prayer chain moving. At that point, we had no idea if Jim and I would be arrested. There was no time to ask any questions.

We left one of our cell phones with our kids and told them what was happening. We told them to stay in the house and not to open the curtains or answer the door. While we didn't want to scare them, we had to tell them that if we didn't come back then they were to call their sister in America and let her know. We assured them that she would take care of the rest.

After that, I ran down to the first foster house and told our American volunteers to go to their apartments and not come out. Because I had no idea what the reason was for the police presence, I had to be sure that the volunteers were safe. I told our manager what was happening, and I instructed her to tell the staff to get the babies ready. I also asked her to go to the next foster house to let the staff know what was happening.

As we were scrambling to get the babies ready, I started praying for God to please keep all of us safe—our children, our volunteers, and our staff. We had no idea why the police were coming. Was it because of our foreign presence? Was it to arrest us? Was it to arrest our staff? Or was it simply to

The Horrible Day

ensure that we did not cause any trouble during the transfer of the children?

At exactly the fifteen-minute mark, my friend from the orphanage came heading towards our door. I ran out to meet her, literally falling into her arms sobbing. There were at least 15 people with her—people with whom I had worked for years at the orphanage. You could see from the looks on their faces that they were just as upset as we were. Several of them started to say, "I'm sorry. I'm sorry." They knew how much we loved the children, and they had witnessed the incredible care we had given them. It was a horrible situation for everyone there.

I stepped inside the door of our first home, and the ayi brought me our first baby. I was sobbing as I kissed her on the cheek, giving her a big hug and telling her how much I loved her. I then passed her off to my friend who in turn gave her to one of the orphanage staff members.

One by one, each child was put into my arms for me to say goodbye. The staff was crying so hard as they called out each of their baby's names. They sobbed as they said goodbye to their precious babies and placed them in my arms before I passed them to the orphanage staff. The orphanage staff was clearly rattled with nervous and upset looks on their faces. No one was saying anything, but chaos ensued, and the babies started to cry from all the confusion.

Once the house was empty, I followed everyone out to the van to finish loading up. They started to close the van door when I said, "No. There are more," and I pointed to our second house. They were stunned. Clearly, they didn't know we had two homes. The Assistant Orphanage Director asked, "Vickie, how many children do you have?" I told her we had eighteen babies, and there were nine other children at our second house. Her eyes widened in surprise.

We went to the other house and repeated what we had just done at the first house. The difference was that this house was home to our older babies and toddlers. The children were terrified. The babies were crying, the ayis were crying and I was crying. It was complete devastation and chaos.

Finally, I held the last baby in my arms. She was one of the original four that we first brought home. She had never been adopted. I walked her out to the van and there in front of me were all the babies that Jim and I once delivered from the orphanage. We had brought each of these children home to a life of love. Now I was forced to put each of them back into the prison they came from, sentencing them to a life of neglect and abuse.

At this point, most of the babies were sweating and most of them were crying. They were so scared and so confused. I tried to find a staff member who had an empty spot on her lap to place the last baby. We finally found a spot for her. I reluctantly placed her in the van, giving her a long hug and kiss and telling her how much I loved her before I let her go.

Jim shut the van door and it pulled away. Jim held me, and we stood there holding each other watching our entire world drive away from us. Once the van was out of sight, we stood there in the middle of the road crying in disbelief at what had just happened. Within thirty minutes we had lost eighteen children. Our entire ministry was over.

Once we pulled ourselves together, we went back to our home to check on our kids. We let them know that we were safe. The police never did show up. We are so thankful that God divinely protected us from the possibility of being arrested. Why didn't the police show up that day? Only God knows.

I then went to the apartment where our manager and

The Horrible Day

two of our US volunteers lived. I needed to make sure they were okay. None of us were able to speak. We just sat there in shock.

The silence broke with a loud ding from my phone. It was a message from my friend at the orphanage. It read, "Vickie, I'm sorry, but our staff does not know who some of the children are. Can you please tell me their names?" Little by little, she sent pictures of our babies for me to identify. Many of the babies were crying, and many were sitting in complete shock. It was horrific to see.

It was one thing for my mind to imagine what they were going through at that moment, but it was entirely different to see it with my eyes. I took my phone and tossed it. I couldn't bear to look at them. The orphanage staff didn't even know who our children were anymore because our kids had blossomed and developed so much in our care.

I cried under my breath as I tried to gather my composure. I retrieved my phone and began pulling up our children's roster which held their Chinese names and birthdates. One by one, I identified our babies.

Afterward, my friend responded back to me with four simple words, "Vickie, I'm so sorry."

The days that followed were very similar to the days following a sudden death. Though our children had not died physically, they had died in our hearts. The grief was unbearable. Our staff and volunteers cleaned out the two foster homes, scrubbing down all the equipment and the floors. They washed all the children's clothes, folding everything and putting them into piles.

I remember the next morning walking to our homes. I saw the children's pajamas which they had worn the night before now laundered and hanging out to dry. Those drying pajamas bitterly hung as a reminder of the many children who had once filled our homes with so much life.

We had not only loss a child to death, but now we had lost every single one of our children to the hands of evil. Sentenced once again to a life of abuse and neglect. Sentenced to a life of rejection and suffering.

Within a few days, the homes were cleaned spotless, and all the children's possessions and toys were stacked in the corners of their rooms. Our homes were once filled with so much love, laughter, and life. Now they sat empty. They were nothing more than empty rooms surrounded by concrete walls. Just like they were before our foster ministry began.

The days following the loss of our children are still very foggy for me. How does a person process the loss of eighteen children? How does a person process the loss of a ministry that only days before was dripping in God's favor?

The nights following that horrific day were long; I rarely slept. When I would drift off to sleep, I had nightmares about our children and what was happening to them.

I thought about Lucy and what her world was like those first few days, weeks and months after losing her family. Our children had no idea what was happening to them, and like Lucy, I knew they were calling for their family to rescue them.

I thought about the saying 'It is better to have loved and lost than to have never loved at all'. Was that really true? Was it better that we had taught our babies to love, or would they had been better off not knowing what they were now missing?

The guilt was unbearable. I blamed myself for being so naïve to think if I followed the law, then it would all turn out alright. I felt so guilty for not protecting them. It was a vicious cycle of guilt and self-condemnation.

In the days and weeks that followed, I found myself going through the mourning process. First, there was the shock. Then sorrow. Then anger. It was such a dark and hard season. Even though I had Jim and my family there with me, I had never felt more alone and confused.

On top of all that, there was the silence we experienced from many of the people in our ministry community. So many of those who had been praying for us now did not know what to say. Most didn't say anything at all. They didn't need to because I knew what they were thinking. They were just as shocked and confused as we were. They too were asking God why He did not intervene. Why God? Why? That single question would haunt me for a very, very long time.

Chapter 9
The Long Journey Back

It was the last day of the month. Our foster homes had been closed for a little over two weeks. It was payday for our staff, and we all gathered one last time for them to receive their final paychecks.

Despite the tears, it was a beautiful time. Together, with the staff and the ayis, we held each other, we laughed, and we cried. It was good to be surrounded by people who were experiencing similar heartache, similar pain, and similar grief.

With our goodbyes looming, we savored each other's company and took lots of pictures. It felt so good to be with those whose hearts were hurting just as much as our own. You know the saying, misery loves company. It's true. We were finally with people who absolutely understood every ounce of our pain and grief. We were able to comfort each other and know that despite the language barrier, grief was universal.

Prior to closing the foster homes and losing our children, our family had already planned a trip back to the States for a time of respite. We had been in China for two years, so it was time to rest and to visit with our families stateside. At the time that we booked our flights, we had no idea just how badly we would need the time away.

About two weeks before it was time to leave for the US, I had been at our manager's home for a meeting. As I was walking back to our house, I saw Jim standing in our courtyard speaking with a Chinese woman. I recognized her as a neighbor in our community. She looked visibly upset. I said hello and then proceeded inside the house.

Jim came in a few minutes later and sat down beside me at the dining room table. I asked what was going on and he said, "Vickie you're never going to believe what she wants. She said her baby girl is very sick and needs medical help that she can only receive in America."

He paused, and then he said, "She wants to give her baby to us. She told me that she knows we are kind people and that we had adopted Chinese children, and she will give her daughter to us and not ask for her back. She only wants her daughter to live." He handed me a piece of paper with the woman's phone number on it.

We always knew that there was the possibility of one day opening our front door to find a baby there. It happened to other organizations who served in China. We had a plan in place if this were to happen, but we didn't have a plan for this.

We knew we couldn't take her baby, but we wanted to learn more to see if we could help her. I called our manager and told her the woman's baby was sick, and since the woman's English was broken, Jim was struggling to put together the pieces. I asked our manager if she would call this woman on our behalf.

About fifteen minutes passed and our manager called me back. She said, "Vickie, she wants to give her baby to you! Can you believe that? She wants to give her baby to you. No strings attached. She said her baby is very sick and needs medical care that Chinese medicine cannot give to her. She promises you can keep her, and she will not take her back." I asked my manager what the baby's condition was, and she said it was spinal muscular atrophy (SMA).

I was familiar with a lot of special needs, but I had never heard of this condition, so I started to research it. It ended up that it was a rare condition of the muscular system with no known cure, and it resulted in a very short life span for the child.

While there was nothing we could do for this sweet baby, we asked our manager to set up a time for Jim and me to visit with the mother and the baby.

It was a very difficult visit. In addition to the mother and baby, the father, their three-year-old son, and the father's parents were all at home.

The mom looked exhausted. She had dark circles under her eyes. We learned that because the baby was seriously ill, the grandparents refused to touch the baby. The baby's father had basically become the primary caregiver of their three-year-old son because mom needed to care for their sick baby around the clock.

The baby girl was absolutely beautiful and gave us a huge smile when she first saw us. We spent well over an hour talking with the mother, our manager serving as our translator. The entire time we were there, the father of the baby paced back and forth while the mother did all the talking. He was wearing so much guilt. He was visibly nervous. We had no idea how much the woman had shared with him prior to our visit. We didn't know if she had made the decision alone to ask us to take her baby or if they had made it together. The parents told our manager that they believed we had come to their home to take their child.

Jim and I took turns holding the baby. She was so precious and oh did it feel good to hold a baby in my arms again. She was so soft and so special.

The Long Journey Back

NEIGHBOR'S BABY

The mother proceeded to tell us that she had been watching our family for a very long time and that it took her weeks to finally approach us. Can you imagine being a parent and wrestling with the decision to give your child to someone? I can't. I absolutely cannot.

We told her how brave she was to come to us, and we knew it took a lot of courage to ask for our help. Then we broke the news to her that we could not take her child, but we would do all we could to help her. We brought with us an oxygen monitor so that she could keep an eye on the baby's oxygen levels. We also brought a swing so that the baby could sit up, allowing her to drain the fluids and congestion in her chest.

The woman shared with our manager that her in-laws were trying to talk her into abandoning the baby so that she would be taken to the orphanage, knowing that ultimately the baby would die there. As our manager shared this with us, my mind went to all the memories of every child I had ever held at the orphanage.

What these families go through to make the decision to leave their children is agonizing. We had been firsthand witnesses to the country's medical care, or lack thereof. It's a cash-based system. If you don't have the money to pay for the services, then the person will die. For many families, abandoning their child is the only hope to get the medical services the child needs, and even that is a very long shot.

For this family, that was not the case. They had the money to pay for the services. However, there simply wasn't anything available to them in China that would help their daughter.

I decided to share my heart with the mother. I told her that she had two choices. She could give up her child, and her baby would die alone in the orphanage. I told the mother that if she abandoned her daughter, she—the mother—would most likely live with regret and guilt for the rest of her life.

Then I gave her another choice. I told her that she could choose to keep her baby and love her and care for her until she took her last breath. I told the mother that this choice would be hard, but she would know that her baby was leaving this world having received so much love from her mama.

The mother held her head down crying as our manager translated this to her. The mother slowly nodded her head in agreement. It was a difficult choice, but I left there with a sense that she was going to keep her baby.

The day came for us to load up and head back to the States for a time of rest. The plan was to be there for two months, and then return to China and begin the process of re-building the ministry.

Our plan was to build a community center for local families who had children with special needs. The center would provide education, therapy and a support system for the families. We thought that if we could provide a place for

The Long Journey Back

these families to receive services then fewer families would make the decision to abandon their children.

We left China the same way that we came. Each of us had a single suitcase filled with our clothes and personal items. When we landed in the US, we literally had only the clothes on our backs. No home. No car. No job. No income. We were returning the same way - just each other and our God. That was enough for us.

We returned to the States and began the next phase of our journey. We left China brokenhearted, and though we didn't realize it at the time, so much more heartache was to come once we returned to the States. The transition was so much more difficult than we expected. We experienced what is called reverse culture shock. Everything was different and nothing felt familiar.

I remember our first morning in the US. I got up before the rest of the family so that I could have my quiet time and a hot cup of coffee. In China, it was not safe to drink the water from our faucets, so we had to use bottled water daily. On this first morning back in the States, I made coffee using running water from the faucet in the kitchen—a luxury I had not had for a very long time.

The home we were staying in had a filter system on the faucet, and I had no idea how to get it to work. As I was trying to figure that out, my phone started making a loud buzzing sound. I literally jumped as I reached for my phone. It was an Amber Alert for a missing child. Not one minute later the faucet started beeping with a flashing light that read, "filter." I was turning in circles, completely unsure what sound to respond to and how to respond to it.

While it sounds silly now, my mind felt like it was in a fog, and I had no idea where I was or what was happening. I'm sure it was a combination of the jetlag and being in a strange place, but at the time I had never felt so confused and so lost. I had no idea what was happening to me. Confusing and lost became our norm as we adjusted to life in the US. Combined with our grief and the overwhelming task of starting over, every day was a tremendous struggle. Soon I found a way to cope: stay busy!

The first few weeks in the States were busy as we spent time with friends and family who wanted to see us. I made appointments for all four of the kids to go to the dentist and eye doctor. It had been two years since they saw specialized doctors. I also took our two children with heart conditions for their necessary checkups and tests.

The busyness of those initial weeks in the US was a much-welcomed distraction. I didn't allow myself to think about China or the babies. I just put one foot in front of the other as I tended to our family's needs.

Once I got over the initial hurdle of figuring out how to work with the many new technologies and luxuries at our disposal, I found myself enjoying the simple things that we had been without for so long such as drinking water from the faucet and talking to people without a translator. My personal favorite was the freedom of being able to jump in the car and drive wherever I wanted to go. No taxi. No public bus. No language barrier. It felt so good to have things easy for once.

Our first visit back to our church was tough. So many people wanted to talk to us, and yet most of them only wanted to talk about China. It was so difficult. I knew it wasn't their fault. They were trying to process and make sense of things as much as we were, but honestly, China was the last thing I wanted to think about or talk about. The pain and grief were too raw; I simply wasn't ready.

Prior to returning to the States, a family offered to let us stay in their vacation home in Florida. What a huge blessing that was for us. After we finished all our appointments and obligations in Ohio, we headed south.

The road trip to Florida afforded us an opportunity that we couldn't pass. We were able to visit with two of the families who had adopted babies from our foster program. The first stop was to visit the family of Mimi. Only God could have orchestrated such a visit. With the frailty of my emotions, I had no idea what to expect or how I would handle it, but I knew I was not going to miss the opportunity to see her if I could.

I remembered Mimi as the tiny baby who I fed with an eyedropper, couldn't make eye contact and had a hollow, dazed expression. I remembered how Mimi perked up when I sang Jesus Loves Me to her, and I remembered how much progress Mimi made in learning to eat. She was a fighter, and now she was with her forever family.

As soon as I saw her my eyes welled up with tears. She was now almost four years old and had grown so much. It was incredible to see her thriving with her family. She was all smiles, and she was busy, busy, busy. The entire time we were with her, she was on the move. She let me hold her a few times, and there was a moment when she looked me square in the eyes. At that moment, I think she remembered me. As we locked eyes, she head-butted me and boy did she get me good.

While she was not able to verbalize what she was feeling inside, I sensed that my presence was upsetting her. I do believe she remembered me, and I think it brought her back to some old feelings and emotions. We were supposed to return the next day for another visit. I asked her mom if we should cancel because I thought I had upset Mimi and I did not want that for her. After talking with her mom, she encouraged us to come back for a final visit the next day.

The second visit went much better than the first. I sat on the front porch of their home in a big rocker watching Mimi play outside. My heart was so full. God was continuing to heal little Mimi. The miracle of what God's love and healing look like was right there before my very eyes. She laughed and played, running all over the yard and riding in her little car. Not only had she survived, but she was healing, and she was growing into the beautiful creation God intended for her to be.

As we continued to travel down to Florida, we made a stop to see another of our babies. She was our very first child with Down syndrome to be adopted from our foster home. She was happy and bubbly, and she gave all of us lots and lots of hugs. Her adoption had been much more recent, and she remembered our entire family. Oh, the joyous reunion we had with her that day.

There are not enough words I can find to explain what it feels like to know your hands were used by God to take a child out of darkness, love them back to life, and then safely deliver them into the arms of their forever family. Our hearts were filled with so much happiness and joy that day. We were so thankful for the time given to us to see two of our precious girls.

We finished our trip down to the very southern tip of Florida, and then we started to settle into our temporary living situation. This would be our home for the next few weeks, and we were so looking forward to the quietness and solitude. We were mentally and emotionally exhausted, and the time had come to finally rest.

Chapter 10

The Battle

When God speaks to me, it is most often through His Word or His Holy Spirit. It wasn't until we moved to China, that God began to also speak to me through my dreams and visions.

It was the morning of our final trip to the provincial government office. It was during this trip that we would learn of the government's final decision that we could no longer keep our babies.

It was 4:30 am and God woke me very suddenly. I was still in bed, completely awake and alert. With my eyes open, I could see the mouth of a lion roaring directly in front of me. The lion's mouth was open so wide that his eyes were all but closed. I was so close to his face that I could barely see beyond his expansive mouth.

Surrounding the lion, on both sides and above him, were swirling streaks of light. The streaks were black and gold lights intertwined and swirling around each other.

I sensed that I was witnessing a battle, and the black and gold lights represented good and evil. The roar that was coming from the lion was fierce and commanding. It was evident that the lion was in complete control of it all. Then I heard God say to me, "The battle is mine."

"THE BATTLE IS MINE" ILLUSTRATION[2]

And just like that, it was all gone—the vision, the lion, and the roar - all of it disappeared in an instant. My assumption at the time was that the message pertained to the battle I was getting ready to go into that day with the government officials.

Fast forward three months later, and I was sitting on the other side of the world in a stranger's home in Florida. We had only been in Florida for a day or two when God reminded me of the vision of the lion and the words that God spoke to me through that vision, "The battle is mine."

Even though I had recorded that vision in my journal, so much had happened in the past three months that honestly, I had forgotten all about it. Now, three months later, I was sitting there reminded of the vision of the lion. God was bringing back this memory, reigniting my soul with the words He had spoken to me on that dreaded morning in China.

I picked up my journal and began searching for the entry. When I found it, I looked at the date. It was hard to believe that I had received that vision only three short

The Battle

months ago. With all that had happened to us, it felt like it had been three very long years. As I began to read the entry, I could feel the tears welling up inside of me. Then I read the words God spoke to me that morning: "The battle is mine."

I sat there as the hot tears began to slowly roll down my cheeks. I was so tired. My heart was shattered, and I had absolutely no idea how God could put the pieces back together again. Yet there He was in that moment reminding me that the battle was His.

I had just come out of a very fierce battle and the only victor I could see was evil. My shield of faith – the very same gear God tells us to carry with us into battle - was now being dragged behind me as I walked off the field battered and utterly defeated. In a single moment, everything I could identify had been destroyed by evil - our ministry, our calling, our sense of purpose, and most importantly, our children. It was all gone and yet God was telling me once again that the battle was His. All I could think was, "Seriously God?"

If you remember, early on in this book, I asked if you would please have the courage to hang in there with me as I shared my journey through a dark season. If you are reading these words right now, then that means you've stayed with me. Can I share with you how very grateful I am to you for doing so?

Do you want to know why I asked that of you? Because when I was walking through some of my darkest hours, I tried to read whatever I could about other people's journeys of grief and suffering. More often than not, I didn't find any clear answers or life-changing advice. Usually, I would read about another person's journey and their story traveled from Point A to Point Z, leaving out the messy middle that brought them to the other side of the journey.

Many of the stories had happy endings. For those whose stories did not have happy endings, they still declared their love for God and His goodness, regardless of the difficult outcome. However, not even one shared in-depth about the raw and honest struggles that brought them to their conclusions of declaring the goodness of the Lord.

It was frustrating.

I remember reading many memoirs and stories that left me with one question of the author, "But how did you get there?" I questioned if there was something wrong with me and my relationship with God because I was struggling so miserably within my season of sorrow and grief.

At times I would find myself questioning my relationship with God. Was it even real? Was it fake and I didn't know it? Was my relationship with Him not strong enough? Not deep enough? Why was I falling so hard, and why couldn't I seem to find my way through the fog? I was so desperate for answers.

When I sensed God calling me to write this book, I did not want one single tear or moment of sadness to go wasted. I did not want one single person to read this and feel the same type of guilt and shame that I felt when I compared my pitiful self to other people's seemingly happy endings. I knew that God wanted to use our story to reach others, and I knew based on my own experience that the only way to do that was to be as open and honest as possible.

In the pages to follow, I will fulfill a promise that I made to God. I promised Him that I would take my heart, place it into my cupped hands and hold it out for Him to use however He chose. Through my openness and transparency, I hope that when you are in the midst of your journey you will never feel like I did—often guilty and ashamed of how I was walking through my suffering. I felt like a total failure because I didn't think anyone else said or thought about the things I did. I especially didn't feel like I was suffering as a Christian should.

So, thank you for your courage. Thank you for staying here with me.

Chapter 11

From Undone To Unglued

Before we arrived in Florida, I had very little time to process everything that had happened. Honestly, I didn't want to process it. I didn't want to think about our babies. It was too raw and too hard.

I knew it was time to rest and allow the healing process to begin. The home in Florida was quiet. There were six of us living there - Jim and I and our four kids. We desperately needed that time of seclusion as a family. There were few distractions, and no one wanted to talk to us about China.

At first, I welcomed the quietness and seclusion. But the newness wore off quickly, and the harsh reality of my new normal was sinking in. I started to have dreams about the children in China, and the influx of silence gave me way too much time to think and remember.

I tried so hard not to think about the babies and what their present-day lives might be like. The inside knowledge I had of the day to day operations of the orphanage used to be such a blessing, but now it felt like a curse.

I thought about the babies laying in their cribs on the wooden boards soaked in urine. I thought about the babies being fed a sludge mixture of ground rice and water. I thought about the babies living these realities day after day after day. My wandering mind haunted me. Were they cold? Were they crying? Were they sick? My mind could not stop thinking about what was happening to them.

Then there was the guilt. It plowed over me like nobody's business. I felt so guilty. I felt like I had failed the children. I felt guilty for filing our paperwork and causing all of this to happen. I felt guilty for not protecting them. I felt guilty for leaving China and enjoying the luxuries of life in America while they were stuck in the orphanage suffering. Then I felt guilty for feeling guilty. It was a vicious cycle.

The sadness hit me like an ocean wave. It just kept coming at me again and again. I had no way of being able to process the guilt and sadness. It was too much. It was too overwhelming. I didn't know where to begin.

On top of my own suffering, I really struggled with how others engaged with me in relation to my suffering. So many people wanted to say something to make me feel better, but their words almost never helped. Often, I ended up in tears, feeling even worse, despite their efforts to encourage me.

I can talk about it now, but at the moment, I felt so unseen, unheard and misunderstood.

Many of the questions we faced included: "When will you get your children back?" "Where did they take your children?" "When will you get to visit your children?" "Well, at least they got to know the love of a family." "But think about all the children you were able to help." "Aren't you happy to be out of that country?" These questions were innocent and well-meaning, but in the depths of my grief, they felt insensitive and painful.

In addition to the numerous questions, many Christians offered us godly advice in an effort to encourage us. We received a lot of the following: "You know God works all things together for His good." "Suffering brings perseverance." "God is in control." "This was His will." "God has His angels watching over them." And one of my all-time favorites (I am being totally facetious), "You know, those children are carrying God's light in that orphanage."

For me, the single hardest question was, "How are you doing?" It made me want to curl up into a ball and cry. How am I doing? Do you really want me to answer that question? It was impossible to articulate how I was doing, and even if I could, the answer would be far from pretty.

The granddaddy question of them all hit my soul deeply. I had a woman ask me, "What happened for God to remove His favor from you?" I kid you not. I had a woman ask me that. Those words and their implications magnified the deep pain, sorrow, and confusion that I was already enduring.

Much like the many questions, the Scripture-based encouragements felt like salt in a wound rather than offerings of peace and strength. I know that most people who reached out to us did so with good intentions, but at the time, their words made me feel even more wounded.

I am not mocking God's Word. His Word is true – it was then, and it is now. But please hear me when I say this: Just because He works good in all things does not mean all things are good.

As I've journeyed through this experience, I walked away from it asking myself a very important question.

As Christians, do we know how to come alongside others who are suffering and provide the support and understanding that they really need during their darkest hour?

When someone we love or care about is suffering, it can be so hard to know what to say or do. Sometimes – many times – it's best to give the broken and the suffering space to just be in their sorrow and in their grief. I'm not suggesting staying away from them, rather give them the space they need to express whatever and whenever they need to.

Instead of offering a word of encouragement, quoting a scripture, or suggesting a silver lining, what might it look like to instead offer the suffering a physical shoulder to cry on without any words? What might it look like to offer them your ear? To listen as they share their hearts no matter the pain, the sorrow, the anger or the rage? What might it look like to just sit with them and be still as they move through the process of experiencing a full range of emotions?

I know it's tempting to want to fill in the awkward white space and uncomfortable silence but know that it's only awkward and uncomfortable for you. Grief is a heaviness that demands space. What might feel uncomfortable for you is likely necessary for the one who is suffering.

While I can talk openly about these things now, at the time the words and comments were so hurtful. I could feel a layer of crust beginning to form over my heart towards people in general. I felt little empathy towards others. I couldn't stomach to read the simplistic whines and complaints of people on social media. Their woes seemed so insignificant compared to what I was suffering.

I was convinced that no one had known suffering like mine. I was certain that no one understood what we were feeling or what we were going through because our situation was unique.

I was in the early days of grief - the anger phase - and the wrath of my emotions were slowly starting to rage inside my heart. As I reflect on the grief that was brewing inside of me during that time, it seems like I was completely self-absorbed. And the truth of the matter is, I was completely self-absorbed. My grief was so debilitating that I had little capacity to think outside of myself. I was sinking and completely weighted down by my sorrow, and I was unable to lift myself out of the quicksand that was sucking me under.

It was also during that time that I woke up one morning to a message from a gal within the adoption community. She had received some updates about a few of our babies in China, and she thought for sure that I would want to see them. Before my very eyes, my worst nightmare became a visible reality. Every ounce of fear and worry I had for our babies was now confirmed in the pictures and videos that she sent me.

I hardly recognized our children. They had lost weight. They had pale white pasty looking skin from malnutrition. They had sores on their faces and heads, and their little eyes were filled with so much sadness. Their souls seemed completely absent. Their joy had been robbed by the treacherous conditions within the orphanage.

One video she sent me was of one of our little girls who had a lot of developmental delays. This little one had been making so much progress with us. When I saw the video of her I burst into tears. Our sweet baby girl was laying in her crib with her tongue hanging out, unable to sit up. She did not at all resemble the little girl who had left my arms just a few months earlier. Anger rose up inside of me, and at that moment, something snapped!

I took a still shot of the video, and I went into my photos to retrieve one of the pictures I had taken of the same girl a few months earlier. I created a side by side photo of her to show a before and after. The transformation was horrific. Only two short months inside of the orphanage and they had sucked the life out of our fragile baby.

BEFORE AND AFTER 2 MONTHS IN ORPHANAGE

I then took the photo and put it on my Facebook page. Along with the photo, I wrote a very long and a very anger filled, righteous ranting about the Chinese government. I spewed on and on about their treatment of their orphans, along with anything and everything that came to my mind. I held nothing back. I was completely undone, and I had become completely unglued.

I had worked in orphan ministry for ten years and never once had I publicly been disrespectful towards the Chinese government. I never publicly said one unkind word. I never did anything that would bring dishonor to their government or their system. But at that moment, my fierce mama heart had all it could take, and I unleashed the fury that had been held captive in my heart for the past two months.

To make matters worse, I held onto that post for a solid 24 hours before posting it. I didn't just write it in haste. I slept on it. I gave the words plenty of thought. I could not even use the excuse that what I posted was a knee jerk reaction. I knew exactly what I was doing.

The next morning, I opened my drafted post, re-read it, and said, "Here ya go Facebook! I am making this post public because I want the whole world to see what they have done to our babies!" My heart was filled with rage as I hit publish.

I closed my computer and that was it. I kid you not, I did not give it a single thought for the rest of the day. I felt one hundred times better because of my release. I had zero regrets, and I slept better that night than I had in a very long time.

The next morning, I rolled over in my bed and looked at my phone to find the time. It was then I discovered several text messages from a few of our board members. They were frantic. "Vic, have you seen Facebook? You've got to take down your post! Take it down now!"

I knew these ladies well enough to know that they were not scolding me. They had walked through the same fire of tragedy that I had. We were a tight-knit team of mama warriors, and they had cried just as many tears over our children as I had.

I could clearly tell from their tone that they were panicked, and when I opened my Facebook page I understood why.

I had over 200 personal messages, several hundred more public comments, and my post had been shared well over 800 times with hundreds of comments from all over the world!

Holy cow! I skimmed through a few of the comments and people were outraged at what had happened to our children. They were ready to call their congressmen. They were ready to contact Beijing. The outcry was loud, and the people were just as angry as I was!

While I had no regrets about sharing that post (and I still don't to this day), I knew there were many organizations continuing to serve orphans in China. My post could have an adverse effect on their programs, especially their ability to continue caring for the orphans.

So, I went to my post and deleted it.

I was done.

That was my tipping point.

I went to my Facebook page and deactivated my account. It was time to check out. Not only from Facebook, but the world as a whole. I was done with social media. I was done with people and their ridiculous comments and questions. I was done trying to put on a brave face when in reality I wasn't brave. I was sinking, and I was sinking quickly.

From that moment on, I made the decision to take control of my personal sphere. This meant that I fiercely controlled what I allowed my heart to see and hear from the outside world. It started with blocking what media I consumed. That meant no more social media and no more local news. Additionally, I only allowed a very limited number of people in my life.

I tightened my inner circle, allowing very few people access to me. Those with whom I remained in relationship included our immediate family, our pastor, one very dear Sister in Christ, our board members and two couples who had limped beside us through our storm. In total, my circle included less than twenty people.

Next, I assigned a spokesperson for me and our family. If someone needed to reach us for any reason, they had to go through this individual. If we needed to get word out to others, we utilized this same person. This was a huge relief for our family and for our ministry.

Please know that everyone's story and process look different, but as I said earlier in this chapter, my goal is to be transparent with the details of my journey. I am by no means a professional counselor, but it is my hope that by being honest and sharing some of the steps I took, might help others as they walk through their own difficult journeys.

For me, the first step was to protect my heart from what and who would have access to it. This helped me stay focused on healing without any more hurt or distractions to interrupt the process.

I also gave myself permission to take these steps and not feel guilty about them. I have never been one to ignore texts and emails, but I had to during that time. There were some people who contacted me saying that they were praying for me or thinking of me. Sometimes I replied with a simple "thank you," but many times I just didn't reply at all. And you know what? That was okay.

The other boundary I set in place was that I made absolutely no commitments during that time. My mind was completely stretched, and I was physically and emotionally exhausted. I had given so much of myself for so long, and there was nothing left inside of me to give. The energy I did have left was reserved for my husband and children. That's it. It was time for me to get better, despite having no idea how I would ever get there.

Chapter 12

Lament

I remember one of the last things our pastor said to me before we left for our respite in Florida. "Vickie, give yourself plenty of time to lament."

I had no idea what that would look like but after my explosion on Facebook, I knew that my pastor was right. If I were going to move through this process in such a way that led to healing and wholeness, lament was probably a pretty good place to begin.

A lifeline to me during this process was undoubtedly God's Word. Though I struggled to stomach the scriptural insights of well-meaning Christians, spending time alone with God's voice through His Word allowed me to meet with Him in my own time and at my own pace.

I began reading through the book of Job, and I found myself shaking my head in disgust at some of Job's supposed friends. Their responses to his suffering struck a chord with me. Job had gone through a series of extreme hardships including the loss of his family, his wealth and eventually his very own health.

At the beginning of his hardships, Job's friends were supportive, doing their best to provide him with comfort. But their support eventually turned into questions and ultimately accusations. They were convinced that Job had surely done something to bring all these painful trials on himself. In trying to make sense of what had happened to Job, his friends grasped for any reason to answer the question, "Why?"

Reading Job's story, I thought, "Wow, I guess humans haven't changed much at all since those days." In our humanness, our minds reach for reasons to justify nearly everything that happens to us. We try to make sense of our situations and circumstances, and we desire order within the often chaotic and disorderly world around us. We default to logic, trying to understand the why behind the things happening to us and around us.

For those who were close to our ministry, they knew that we had a growing, thriving program. They watched as we cared for orphans, sometimes even saving their lives, and these same ministry partners watched as we were forced to give back every single one of our precious children. Just like us, our partners and supporters knew that our children were returning to a life of neglect, abuse, trauma, and horror.

When these dear children were forced out of our homes and back into the orphanage, we all sat in shock, anger, discouragement, and disbelief. Jim and I weren't the only ones asking questions of God. Just like us, those close to our ministry also wondered where God was in all of this? Why didn't He answer our prayers? Why didn't He save those innocent babies? Why did He allow this to happen? Why did He allow evil to have victory over His ministry for His children?

Like Job's friends, when things didn't make sense, many of the people around us came up with their own logical reasons for what happened. I did the same thing in trying to make sense of a seemingly senseless situation. Many of the questions that others were asking were the very same questions that I had been wrestling with since the day that the orphanage vans drove away from our foster homes with our precious babies inside of them.

I knew the promise of God's comfort and His peace. I knew that God works all things together for our good. But what I didn't know was why it felt like those prayers were hitting a glass ceiling and bouncing right back to me. It felt as though God was completely silent.

What does one do when God's promises don't penetrate the heart? Where is God in the darkness, and how do I get back to Him? He promises me He will never leave me or forsake me, but where is He now in my suffering? How do I get back to having faith and trust in a God who seems to have disappeared on me?

Those were the questions on my heart. Those were the questions for which I needed answers.

When you love someone and have a good relationship with them, you feel safe to say and do things that you would never dream of saying or doing with anyone else. Jim, my best friend and husband of over three decades, is that safe person in my life. I considered my relationship with God equally as safe.

It was in that safe place that I spewed out my most hurtful and anger filled expressions of grief and lament. I have literally shaken my fist in the air while crying out to God, "Give me back my babies! You could have stopped this, and you didn't! Why? Why would you let those innocent babies suffer and be abused when you could have stopped it? Why God? Where are you? Do you even care? Are you even listening? Do you not realize how many people are watching and waiting for you to show up? Why didn't you?

You are blowing it big time! You've failed these babies. You've failed your own ministry, and you've failed me! I thought you loved them. I thought you loved me. God, I trusted you! You have betrayed me. You have betrayed my faith in You. God . . . I trusted you. I trusted you. I trusted you!"

I kicked and fought as I tried to make sense of it all. My human mind could not grasp the meaning of the madness that was happening to me and around me. I wrestled God to the ground with all my questions. I needed it all to make sense. No, actually, I demanded it.

For several months I carried on, trudging through my battle of grief and lament. Then one day I just stopped.

I was exhausted. I laid barren, battered, and bruise and I could no longer fight. I was finished. It was at that moment that I remembered the words that God had whispered to my heart, "The battle is mine."

I took what shattered pieces of my heart were left and I laid them out before Him. I said, "Okay God, I give up. There is nothing left inside of me. I can no longer fight this battle. If you are still here. If you can hear me. If you are even interested in what's left of this broken vessel, it's Yours. I give to you what tiny crumbs of faith that I have left, and I'm holding them up to You in outstretched hands. I have no idea if it's even enough, but it's all I have left to offer."

It wasn't a pretty prayer. There were no fireworks or bright lights. It was simply a raw moment of honesty. A prayer of lament as I lay in utter brokenness and defeat.

Again, I share all of this with you in an effort to be completely transparent. Most of these words were taken straight out of the journal that I kept during that difficult and dark season. You may find the words hard to read, but

I can assure you that they were even harder for me to write and ultimately publish for the whole world to see.

But I knew I had to be completely honest with what my lament looked like as it came straight from my heart to God's. My words are important because I believe that the lament process is one of the most important and necessary steps in the healing process.

By sharing my honest feelings and emotions with Him, I unknowingly invited God to be with me in the very depths of my grief.

Journaling and prayer allowed me to take the feelings that were inside of me and transfer them to the hands of God. God was and is fully able and fully willing to hold them for me as I walked through my journey of grief.

My heart had been shattered into a thousand pieces, and I had no idea how He would ever make it whole again. My faith had been rocked to the core. What was once a very close and intimate relationship with God was now no more than a simple question, "Who are You and where are You?"

That may sound like a strange thing to say, but it was the question that I had to ask. Never had this been my experience of God. I had never experienced a time when He felt completely absent and removed. His presence had always been with me, loving on me and comforting me in every situation of my life. We had walked through so many highs and lows together, but now I didn't know how to find my way back to Him. I felt completely and utterly lost and alone.

Maybe you have lost a child or you are living in an abusive marriage. Maybe you have lost a loved one to illness or accident. Maybe you are dealing with addiction, suicide, or a devastating health report. A prodigal child or infidelity. Whatever the situation, loss, or grief. You know in your heart that God could have stopped it or changed it. Yet He didn't.

You've prayed and maybe even fasted. You've asked others to intercede in prayer for you. Yet God remains silent, and the grief and suffering continue. The prayers go seemingly unanswered and you ask yourself the same question. "God, where are you?"

How does one go from these moments of desperation and grief and find your way back to the safety of His presence, believing and trusting in Him again?

Everyone has a different experience of faith. Everyone has persevered through different circumstances. Everyone's story of loss or injustice looks different. The journey to not only survive, but also to heal and become whole again will be different as well.

There are no easy answers and no secret formulas for healing and wholeness. But what I have learned is that no matter how lost you are in the darkness; God exists without even the smallest expectation of how you should move through your suffering. He doesn't show up only when you suffer in a certain "godly" way. Rather He shows up despite how ugly things might look on your end. No matter how you lament, He is there.

Most of all, He does not expect you to carry the burden or bear the responsibility of healing on your own. That is His job and His alone. The battle is truly His and not yours to fight.

With that being said, you do have a part to play in your healing and restoration. That is where I was struggling the most. I no longer had the faith or the trust inside of me to move. I was completely and utterly frozen in my own prison of grief, unable to take a step toward Him of any kind.

The only tangible thing I could do was open His word.

Lament

Even though the words that were deposited into my heart were like those of a coin being dropped into a bottomless pit, I still read them. Every morning, with coffee in hand, I made my pathetic attempt to read God's Word. Sometimes I read only a few verses, and other times I simply read a short devotion.

No matter what I read during those early mornings, the words seemed to bounce right off my heart and down into that bottomless pit. I was so angry at God. I was so full of mistrust. The crust that had formed over my heart had hardened, and nothing seemed to penetrate it.

On one particular night during that season, our family enjoyed a movie night together, something we loved doing as a family. The kids selected a movie based on a true story about a school shooting that took place within an Amish community. I remembered when the actual event had occurred, so I was curious to watch the movie.

In short, a gunman enters an Amish schoolhouse and shoots several victims, killing several young girls. After the horrific incident, the Amish community learned that the man who shot the girls was a local "English" man whom they all knew and who had lost his own daughter several years earlier.

After he killed the girls at the school, the man took his own life, leaving behind his wife and their other children.

The movie was about the story of the Amish community's forgiveness towards the gunman and the love they showed his surviving wife and family. The lesson of the story was that even after suffering the most traumatic of losses, there is still a path that can lead you forward. The movie asked the question: When God chooses not to intervene, even knowing the consequences will devastate many lives, how can you possibly still move forward?

The gunman was full of anger and hate towards God because of the death of his own daughter. His heart was eaten alive, and he died from the inside out. His tragedy destroyed him. It destroyed his marriage and his family. As his wife surmised in the movie: He chose hell over life with her and his family.

The contrast to his choice was the path that the Amish community took. They chose love, compassion, and forgiveness both for the man and God. They chose faith. They chose to trust God in the promises of His Word and the wisdom of His ways. It didn't change the outcome - their daughters were not coming back, but they chose to seek God amidst the unchangeable circumstances. Their hearts chose life whereas the gunman's heart had died long before he ended his own life.

There was no happily-ever-after to their stories. Both families lost loved ones in a violent and evil manner. They were left to live out their lives with this extremely dark and difficult chapter forever a part of them.

The next morning after watching the movie, I sat staring at my Bible. Instead of reading as I usually did, my mind couldn't stop thinking about the movie. God was working in my heart, and I knew it. For the first time in a very long time, I could sense His presence hovering over me, and honestly, it felt so good. He wasn't saying anything, but I knew He was there with me in that moment. I began to recognize a sense of hunger for His mysterious presence and a desire for Him that I had not experienced in a very long time.

I picked up my Bible and cautiously leaned in. I whispered, "Okay God, I'm listening." I opened my Bible to Isaiah and read, "If you do not stand firm in your faith, you will not stand at all." (Isaiah 7:9) I could feel my heart start to quiver.

At that moment I knew that I had arrived at a fork in the road. Either I was going to believe that God was sovereign and still in charge of the universe, or I was not. Either I was going to believe that God was in control of the uncontrollable or I was going to believe that everything I had ever known about Him simply was not true.

I knew in my heart that if I did not choose to stand up and fight for my healing, I would end up just like that father in the movie. I would end up angry and bitter, and eventually dying from the inside out.

It was time. It was time to stand firm in my faith or not stand at all. It was time to either get busy living or get busy dying.

That morning, I did my part. I took a step – a small step - toward God in my healing and restoration. It started with a very simple prayer. I told God, "Okay, I don't really trust you right now, but I am willing to give you just a tiny piece of my heart. I will give you my first step—a small step of trust. I will choose to stand. The battle is yours."

I had no idea what exactly my prayer meant. I didn't know where to start. I honestly didn't know what to do next. As simple as it was, that prayer was all I could offer up to Him at that moment. I closed my Bible, went out to my husband Jim and said, "I need to get better. I'm ready to contend for my healing. Will you pray for me?"

Chapter 13

Entering The Hidden Place

It was the very next day after I offered up that simple prayer to God and asked Jim to pray for me. I started my day just like always. I got my coffee and headed back to my room to read my Bible just like I did every morning. I started off this morning by reading a short devotional that I received via email. It took me to the book of Hosea. When I finished reading the devotion, I decided to read more from Hosea.

"Therefore, I am now going to allure her; I will lead her into the wilderness and speak tenderly to her. There I will give her back her vineyards and will make the Valley of Achor a door of hope. There she will respond as in the days of her youth, as in the day she came up out of Egypt." (Hosea 2:14-15)

Though the room was completely silent, I had a sense that something was stirring. I stopped my reading, sitting very still. The sense that something was about to happen seemed to be intensifying. My heart began to race. Then I heard it – a whisper. God's soft voice speaking to my heart, "Come away with me to The Hidden Place."

I gasped. Though merely a whisper, the voice was so clear yet so mysterious. "The Hidden Place," I thought,

Entering The Hidden Place

"What is that and where is it? I've heard of the wilderness as mentioned in these verses, but The Hidden Place, what could that mean?"

I looked down and re-read the first verse again. "Therefore, I am now going to allure her; I will lead her into the wilderness and speak tenderly to her." God seemed to be highlighting the phrase, "I am now going to allure her. I will lead her..." I felt a nudge on my heart as if God was affirming what I recognized as His voice. I sat still, silent and in awe.

I had no idea what The Hidden Place was, but what I did know was I had heard His voice very clearly for the first time in a very long time. I was so ready to be with Him and experience Him again.

While my heart felt completely empty of any faith or trust, deep down inside the very crevices of my soul I knew that I was safe with Him. Though I still didn't know exactly what God was asking of me, my heart was ready for this next step. Sitting there alone, I answered Him out loud, "Yes, I'll go away with You."

Simultaneous to my lament and grief process, things in China seemed to be escalating. The government had shut down our programs inside of the orphanage and all our organization's staff had been removed.

The doors of cooperation remained tightly shut. Not only were the doors to orphan aid closed, but the doors to any foreign organizations providing aid inside China were being shut as well. I once heard a pastor say, "When the favor is gone it's time to move on." As quickly and swiftly as God had opened the doors for us to serve in China, He had closed them.

With a heavy heart, it started to become evident to us that our time in China was over. The opportunity to further serve orphans and their families appeared to be a firmly closed door.

Why would God ask us to give away everything and move to China, only to turn us around and move us back two years later? It didn't make sense, and I had to come to the realization that I would probably never have any answers to these questions on this side of heaven.

As we realized that our time in China was permanently over, Jim and one of the men from our church flew over to pack up what personal items of ours they could, giving the rest away. I cannot imagine what it was like for Jim to return to our life in China. I remember the first morning after our babies were gone. I was walking down to the baby house and saw their pajamas hanging out to dry. The homes were empty. The toys were untouched. The cribs were empty. There was only silence. It was eerily sad, and my heart still aches at the thought of it.

Now Jim had to return to the sadness and begin the arduous process of packing up the homes. Jim hired some local men to load all of the babies' equipment, clothing and toys into trucks. They were being donated to the few foreign organizations that were still operating foster care in China. We wanted to be sure that our children's things would be used by other children who needed them.

When I think about how hard it must have been for Jim to go through the process of packing everything up and closing the homes, all I can do is cry. He has always been my hero, and he has always known how to protect my heart. Jim knew that there was no way that I could have handled going back into China. He knew that I could not have handled seeing our children's things again. Oh, how I love that man and the way he loves me so fiercely. I cannot imagine having gone through this life without him.

I remember the morning I received his call from the other side of the world. He had not even been in China a week, packing and giving away all our things. He was scheduled to fly back to the States early the next morning. He called and said only two words to me. "It's done."

"There is a time for everything and a season for every activity under the heavens:
A time to be born and a time to die,
A time to plant and a time to uproot,
A time to kill and a time to heal,
A time to tear down and a time to build,
A time to weep and a time to laugh,
A time to mourn and a time to dance,
A time to scatter stones and a time to gather them,
A time to embrace and a time to refrain from embracing,
A time to search and a time to give up,
A time to keep and a time to throw away,
A time to tear and a time to mend,
A time to be silent and a time to speak,
A time to love and a time to hate, a time for war and a time for peace."
(Ecc. 3:1-8)

Chapter 14
Weariness And Whispers

One of my favorite characters in the Bible is Elijah. He was one of the great prophets in the Old Testament. Even though he had a pretty crummy message for the people of Israel (Elijah prophesied that if God's people did not return to Him, they would face inevitable judgment), he was a steady and obedient servant of God. No matter how bazaar God's request was of him, Elijah obeyed and followed God's commands.

My absolute favorite Biblical story involving Elijah is his showdown with the gods of Baal on Mount Carmel. You can read about this in 1 Kings 18:19-46.

I love this dramatic story of God's faithfulness, and Elijah's victory in this amazing showdown.

The morning that God invited me to go away with Him to The Hidden Place, He prompted me to remember the rest of this story with Elijah.

After all that God had done through His servant Elijah, Jezebel was furious. She was determined to have Elijah destroyed. Elijah literally ran for his life, eventually seeking solace under a bush. There, under the bush, Elijah had an honest conversation with God. Elijah had done everything that God had asked of him, and Elijah was tired. He just wanted to die. "I have had enough, Lord. Take my life." (1 Kings 19:4)

God responded and met Elijah under that bush by sending an angel to feed him. The angel gave him water and hot baked bread so that he had enough nourishment to continue. With God as his provider, Elijah found the strength to continue his travels, ending up in Horeb, the mountain of God. There he went into a cave and spent the night.

I think it's important to note that while in the cave, the Lord came to Elijah. Elijah didn't go to God, rather God went to him. God knew the condition of Elijah's heart and all that Elijah had been through.

God asked him, "What are you doing here, Elijah?" (1 Kings 19:9)

In response to God's question, Elijah laments, pouring his heart out to God. Obviously, God already knew what had happened to Elijah and why he was hiding in a cave. But our Father wants to hear our hearts. Remember what we've learned in the lament chapter? Just like a parent wants their child to share with them when they are hurting or troubled, God desires the same for His children. He loves you and wants you to share what you are feeling and thinking with Him.

God responds to Elijah, with a surprising request. God instructs Elijah to go out of the cave and stand, stating that God's presence would be passing by.

First, a powerful wind passed. Then there was an earthquake followed by fire. But the Lord was not in any of them.

After the fire came a gentle whisper. When Elijah heard it, he pulled his cloak over his face and went out and stood at the mouth of the cave. At that moment, among all the madness and noise of what was happening, Elijah knew God enough to recognize His voice in a simple whisper.

When someone whispers to you, you must lean into them to hear what they have to say. Whispering requires an intimate closeness. Despite all that had happened to Elijah, he knew God intimately, and he recognized God's voice. Elijah leaned into His loving Father to meet with Him.

As I entered The Hidden Place, I leaned towards Him. In His gentleness, He whispered to me one simple word: "Rest."

The first lesson God wanted to teach me in The Hidden Place was that it was time for me to rest.

We had served orphans in China for over a decade, with the last two years being boots on the ground, in the trenches, and on the front lines.

We were weary.

Jim and I had run hard, literally serving those precious children 24/7. Our phones were never turned off. We took turns every other night being on call. With over twenty children, we rarely experienced a night in which we didn't receive a call from one of the nighttime ayis about a sick or sleepless baby.

I remember one night my oldest daughter, who was on the other side of the world and in an opposite time zone, texted me in the middle of the night. When I immediately answered her message she asked, "What are you doing awake? I sent this so that you'd see it in the morning." I responded simply, "Twenty-two babies."

We were always on. We were never able to clock out. We lived and breathed the ministry. Whether we were dealing with staffing, struggling with getting supplies for the children, or meeting our monthly budget, we carried a tremendous amount of responsibility.

But the hardest part of what we did was the responsibility of the children's health and the decisions we had to make almost daily on their behalf. The little clinic where we took our children for medical treatment was a hole in the wall, literally. It was run by an elderly female doctor who would treat our children for us.

The doctor was a Christian woman and she never charged us for her services, only for the medicine that she gave us. But everything was, of course, Chinese medicine so I always took my manager with me to translate. I would have to ask so many questions not knowing what the doctor was giving to our children and why.

The medicine and practices were just so different from western medicine. I would see women in the alley beside the clinic sitting on the ground. While holding a baby in one arm she would hold in the other hand a rusty pole with an IV bag hanging from it. An IV that was attached to the baby she was holding. All of this taking place in the middle of a dirty alleyway. In most cases, this was the best a parent could do or afford for their child.

Almost daily we were making decisions for our children's health. I had one baby almost die in my arms. The stress from the responsibility we had for their medical needs was just incredible.

Then there were the many years of working inside the orphanage before us moving to China full time. My eyes witnessed such horrific things - trauma and tragedy that I will never be able to unsee. I watched children suffering from all types of medical conditions such as a baby whose cleft lip and palate were so severe that half her face was missing. I'll never forget her eyes looking up at me as she lay there with her little tongue making a sucking motion. She was starving to death because she was physically incapable of eating because her mouth was so malformed.

I had staff bring dying babies and place them into my arms, pleading and begging me to save them.

I saw children born with missing limbs, eyes, ears and even bones.

We witnessed children being mistreated and abused. Children who had gone without baths for months.

We met children who were tied up like dogs. Children with their ankles and wrists tied to their beds. We heard the screams of children being beaten. We would even witness children touching other children in inappropriate ways because of what they had either witnessed or experienced themselves.

My mind was full, and my heart was even fuller. My eyes had seen abuse, suffering and injustice. My hands had held death and hopelessness.

I had stuffed so many years of horror as far down into my soul as I could pack it. The loudest of music piped into my ears, and the hottest of showers were only a temporary method of masking the pain.

I felt as if I was literally dying from a broken heart.

I would later be told it was called second-hand trauma.

Chapter 15
Healing Through Tears

True healing would have to come from God Himself. Going away with Him to rest in The Hidden Place would be the first step in my healing journey.

Those early days in The Hidden Place were mostly spent with me sitting in stillness and silence. I played a lot of Christian music, often simply instrumental songs without any words. I never had much to say to God in The Hidden Place, rather I would just sit in His presence and let Him be God to me.

My heart was so tender and fragile. There were times that I would start crying without knowing why. There were tears—so many tears. I would often cry in an instant as if someone had turned on a switch to my tears.

Sometimes I wouldn't be thinking about anything, and then suddenly I would feel the tears welling up inside. Honestly, it was so hard to be in The Hidden Place at first because I had absolutely no control over the tears. My tenderness and fragility were overwhelming.

I soon began to realize that this was part of the process of being in The Hidden Place with Him. After all the years of experiencing second-hand trauma, I was filled with endless memories both tragic and traumatic. God seemed to be surfacing each of them little by little. As a memory would emerge, more tears would fall. It felt as if He was siphoning the tears from my eyes and in doing so, He was emptying my soul and my mind of all that I had been carrying and had stuffed for so many years

There were times that I would look at my hands and I would think of the death and suffering that they had held and touched. Such realizations would cause me to burst uncontrollably into tears. The sorrow just flowed out of me. Day after day I sat at His feet in The Hidden Place with my head on His lap. All I could do was cry. I rarely said anything. I just cried.

Tears are such a powerful thing, and I am so thankful that God gave them to us. They have the power to heal your heart as they flush out your emotions. Whether it be anger or sadness, joy or fear, your tears serve as a sort of healing rinse. They are God's elaborate provision to us through our journeys of healing and wholeness.

In God's infinite wisdom, another of the little gems He placed in His word was to make sure we knew that even Jesus wept while He was living on this earth. That's how important tears are to God.

If you grew up as a child going to Sunday school as I did, you probably know the story of Lazarus. Jesus miraculously restores Lazarus to life four days after Lazarus' death.

Scripture tells us that Jesus visited Lazarus' sisters four days after Lazarus was dead and buried. "When Mary reached the place where Jesus was and saw him, she fell at his feet and said, 'Lord, if you had been here, my brother would not have died.' When Jesus saw her weeping, and the Jews who had come along with her also weeping, he was deeply moved in spirit and troubled. 'Where have you laid him?' he

Healing Through Tears

asked. 'Come and see, Lord,' they replied. Jesus Wept." (John 11:32-35)

Many know the words, "Jesus wept," because it is the shortest verse in the Bible. Many highlight the fact that Jesus was so grief-stricken over his friend Lazarus' death, that he mourned for him.

But I'm not sure that is necessarily the case. Jesus was God, and He knew what was about to happen. He knew beforehand that Lazarus was going to die, and He also knew that He was going to raise Lazarus from the dead. Jesus was and is God; He knows the past, present, and future of all things.

So why did Jesus weep? I believe that Jesus wept less because He was mourning His friend Lazarus and more because He loved His friends Mary and Martha. Though Jesus loved Lazarus, Jesus knew that Lazarus would be raised from the dead. I believe Jesus wept because His friends, Mary and Martha, wept, and He knew that they were hurting.

When I held Mimi, that precious baby who I had to feed in tiny doses with an eyedropper, I could not control the tears that would flow from my eyes. Goodness, I couldn't even look at that sweet baby girl without crying. God's love flowing from me was so radical for that hurting and broken baby that my heart grieved for her with uncontrollable tears.

I believe that God grieves for all of us when we are hurting and suffering in our grief. As God sat with me in The Hidden Place, there were times when I would just sit and cry. I knew in my heart that He was sitting there and crying along with me. I could sense His presence as He wiped my tears away. I could feel His gentleness and compassion as He held me, comforting me with His love.

When Jesus came to this earth, He was still a man in

every sense of the word. He had flesh. He had feelings and emotions just like we do. He felt hunger. He felt thirst. He felt joy. He felt sadness. He felt anger. He felt compassion. He felt grief, and He felt pain.

He knew the joy of friendship and the disappointment of betrayal. He knew and experienced injustice. He knew the sting of rejection. He knew the heartache of one who has been denied by his very own chosen people. I believe that Jesus felt fear and sorrow and pain as he endured beatings, torture and finally a crucifixion to a cross. Jesus was human. He even asked God if His destiny could be changed, ultimately submitting to God's final decision.

Jesus endured the cross, and then He experienced His final moment as a human being. He experienced death.

There is nothing that you feel or experience in this world that Jesus did not experience firsthand. What a beautiful picture of God's perfect provision for us, that our hearts can find comfort in a God who understands as you walk through this sin-filled earth. You can never say to God, "You just don't understand!" Because He does understand—more than you can comprehend.

The enemy would tell me the lie that no one understood the loss that I had endured. The enemy tried to convince me that even God didn't understand my suffering. But I know that is absolutely not true. God saw every time that our children were mistreated, abused, neglected and forgotten. God's eyes saw every single moment of evil that was done to them, and He still sees all of it even in this very moment as you are reading this book.

I was able to take my understanding that God is all, sees all and knows all and apply it to my heart. God did know and He did understand, and that is why he took me away to The Hidden Place. He took me there so that He could sit and cry with me, and the same holds true for you.

God does see your pain. He knows and understands your suffering. He can bring healing if and when you are ready to allow Him to do so. All it takes is the smallest step of trust as you lean into Him. Even if you have no idea how you are going to get to the place of ever feeling whole again, God can move mountains in your life with even the tiniest seed of faith.

Chapter 16

The Soil Of My Soul

"Come near to God, and He will come near to you." (James 4:8)

When God invited Elijah to step out of the cave to meet with Him, it was up to Elijah to take the next step. God promises to come near to you as you come near to Him, a dance that is both an invitation and a mystery.

God is God and we are (wo)man. God doesn't control you like a puppeteer controls a puppet; God loves you way too much for that. This dance of drawing near to God and God drawing near to you is called free will. While He loves you unconditionally, you get to choose whether you take a step toward Him.

After losing our babies and the ministry, silence became a permeating force in my life. It was during those moments of silence that I often found myself asking God, "Where are you?" Just because God is silent does not mean He is absent. His Word promises that He will never leave us or forsake us. (Deut. 31:6)

The longer I sat with Him in The Hidden Place the more I started to realize that He was silent because He knew my heart was not ready to hear what He had to say.

He was right. I wasn't ready. I was mad, and I wanted

to stay mad. To be completely honest, as much as I said I wanted to hear from Him, the truth was that I didn't. I didn't want to hear anything He had to say because I wanted to stay angry, and God, as my loving Father, knew that was the condition of my heart.

Looking back at that time I imagine God standing beside me while compassionately watching and listening to my rants and raves. Like a parent standing near their two-year-old as they throw themselves down on the floor in the middle of the store, God stood by me and let me have my fit.

Just like the tantrum-filled toddler kicks and screams to communicate his/her emotions, I was sulking, shutdown, and hard-hearted as an expression of my sorrow and devastation.

God allowed me to carry on for as long as He knew I needed. Much like a toddler becomes so upset to the point of crashing fast asleep, I too had reached my exhaustion point.

It was then that my loving Father reached down and scooped me up, inviting me to rest and asking me the same question that He asked Elijah, "What are you doing here?"

I was so consumed with the shock and grief of what we had endured, and I just needed some time to be angry. I was a whirlwind of questions, demanding answers for all the injustice that I had witnessed over the years. I was in no position to hear anything that God had to say to me until my fits were over. It was then that I had the capacity to listen.

When Father took me away to The Hidden Place, I was weary, battered, and beaten from the wounds of life's battle. As I stepped into His presence, He scooped me up into His gentle and loving hands. At times I simply cried, sitting at

His feet with my head in His lap. Other times I rested in His tight embrace.

Sometimes, we both cried. I sensed His grief and sadness as He wiped my tears away. Never once did He leave me, and never once did I feel alone in The Hidden Place. I had willingly agreed to meet Him there, and His loving and comforting presence met me with welcome arms.

Much like when I sat and cried with Lucy as she waited on that orphanage floor for her mama, God sat with me. Neither of us said anything, however, we both understood the conditions of each other's hearts.

One morning, as I was sitting with God and reading my Bible, I came across a verse in Hosea, "Sow righteousness for yourselves, reap the fruit of unfailing love, and break up your unplowed ground; for it is time to seek the Lord, until he comes." *(Hosea 10:12)*

The verse gave me pause. I read it again and then again. Once again, I sensed that God wanted my attention. I could feel His presence in such a way that I knew He was getting ready to show me something. I sensed Him highlighting the words, "break up your unplowed ground."

My thoughts immediately went back to the cornfields that surrounded our Ohio farm when I was a little girl. I loved to explore the fields in the springtime. At the end of winter, before anything was planted in the fields, the ground remained hard, with big clumps of dirt leftover from the previous fall's harvest. The dirt clumps were so hard and dense that I had to be very careful walking in the field otherwise I could easily turn an ankle. Even though the clumps were made up of only dirt, the rain would come and go, never breaking up the solid mass. Instead, rainwater would roll off the dirt clumps as if rolling off a rock.

When it was time to plant the fields the next spring, my

The Soil Of My Soul

dad would take his plow and begin churning up the dirt. He started by plowing the entire stretch and breadth of the field. When he was finished plowing, he'd plow it again. It took several rounds with the plow before all the dirt and leftover corn stalks were finally broken up. After all that, he switched machines, putting away the plow and moving to the disk. The disk further processed the dirt that had been plowed. It turned the dirt into the softest, finest soil that you could imagine. The result was an entire field of potting soil.

I loved to go out and stand in the middle of the field while taking in a big deep breath. There is nothing better than the smell of freshly plowed earth. I would sit down and run my hands back and forth through the soil as if it were sand. It felt so soft and so cool. I would form a scoop with both of my hands, fill them with soil, and then I let the dirt slide through my fingers. It felt so good.

Through the plowing and disking process, the lumps of rock-hard dirt were made ready to receive the seeds which would eventually produce that year's harvest.

These memories of my childhood farm took me to the story of Ruth in the Bible. After suffering the loss of her husband, Ruth traveled with her mother-in-law to her mother-in-law's home country. Ruth was not only a foreigner in the land, but she was also a widow.

In those days, widows were without means to support themselves. Without employment, life insurance, or government programs, most widows had to depend on the community or other surviving family members to provide for their housing, or even a simple meal.

A local farmer, Boaz, had mercy on Ruth and decided to take care of her. "So Boaz said to Ruth, 'My daughter, listen to me. Don't go and glean in another field and don't go away from here. Stay here with the women who work for me. Watch the field where the men are harvesting and follow along after the women. I have told the men not to lay a hand on you. And whenever you are thirsty, go and get a drink from the water jars the men have filled.' At this, she bowed down with her face to the ground. She asked him, 'Why have I found such favor in your eyes that you notice me—a foreigner?'" (Ruth 2:8-10)

I can picture Ruth bowing low and putting her face to the ground. I can imagine what that must have felt like as I recall memories of the soil in which I spent so much time playing as a child. I wonder what the soil felt like to her as she bowed humble, pressing her face into the earth.

As I read my Bible that morning, starting in Hosea and then landing in Ruth, I re-read Ruth's question, "Why have I found such favor in your eyes that you notice." Sitting there in The Hidden Place, I could feel my heart begin to quiver, "Why God? Why have you noticed me? Why have you chosen me?"

Ruth's question was my question. As I sat there with God, I could sense His presence speaking grace to my heart. I had been through so much. I had made so many mistakes. I had failed so many times. I had nothing special to offer. Yet He saw me. He knit me together in my mother's womb (Psalm 139:13). He chose me. Why?

Digging deeper into Ruth's questions, I looked up other translations. Each one exactly echoed the cry of my own heart:

"Why should you be so concerned about me?" (GNT)
"Why are you so good to me?" (CEV)
"Why have you been so kind to notice me?" (NCV)
"Why do you care about me?" (NLV)
"Why have I found favor in thine eyes?" (KJV)

With each translation of the question, the answer is the same: Grace. Grace is the answer. God is good to you and me because God is good. God loves you and me because God is love. God sees you and me because He never takes His eyes off His own. God promises you and me that He will never leave us or forsake us.

So why has He chosen me? Certainly, I'm a mess. I've made so many mistakes. Yet He chose me before I was born despite knowing all the times I would fail. His mercy covers the mistakes of my past, and His grace leads me into my future.

I sat quietly for a while as I let these truths sink into my heart. My mind meditated on the scriptures that He had given me, and I reflected on all the things that His Holy Spirit had prompted me to remember from my childhood.

I could feel new questions starting to rise within me. For the first time in a very long time, my questions did not stem from a place of anger, rather they were questions coming from the heart of a daughter to the ears of a loving Father.

I was ready to speak to Him as I drew close to Him in the safety of The Hidden Place.

One of the first questions I asked Him didn't have anything to do with what happened to our children or the circumstances that took us away from China so abruptly. Rather the question I asked God was, "Why had I fallen so hard?"

Over the past decade, my relationship with God had grown into something far richer and intimate than it had ever been before. The last few years in ministry and serving Him in China had deepened my faith in leaps and bounds. I spent hours with Him in prayer and in His word. I did this not because it was the good Christian thing to do, but because

I couldn't get enough of Him. It was no longer a religion for me. It was a relationship.

I was learning who He really was. I was learning how He operated in my life. He was teaching me the power of His Holy Spirit. He was teaching me how to hear His voice. I grew so deeply in love for His children, the poor, the hurting and the lost. He taught me that my identity was in Him. He defined me not by my past or how the world viewed me, rather He taught me how to see myself through His compassionate eyes.

I knew what He had called us to do when we first inclined our hearts towards orphans and China. I heard His voice and I trusted Him with absolute one hundred percent abandonment. There was not a single doubt in my mind that He would provide for us and our children when we followed Him across oceans.

I had zero regrets about giving everything away when we decided to move abroad as a family. In truth, I was excited to follow Him so faithfully. My attitude was "That's just a bunch of stuff we gave away, and in return, we get to be the hands and feet of Jesus to the least of these. Nothing is better than that!" I was all in!

So, when everything started to unravel and the ministry ended as quickly as it started, we were all left scratching our heads in wonder and confusion. What on earth was happening? Nothing made sense, and I was left feeling abandoned by the God whom I loved so deeply.

Once I began to sit with God safely tucked away in The Hidden Place, my heart softened. My grief and my mourning shifted, and it was time to ask God the even bigger questions that were on my heart. Why did I fall so hard? Was there a crack in the dam of my faith that caused it to be so weak that it inevitably broke?

It was time to allow God to plow up the soil of my heart as He pulled me into His lap to begin the process of revealing to me the answers to these questions.

Allowing God to dig up the soil of my soul was another important process of my healing journey, and it can be for you too. When soil is being dug up for planting, what is exposed are rocks, weeds, and anything else that will prevent the seed from taking root and growing.

While none of us want to think about growth in the middle of our healing journey, if you will allow God to, He will use your season of grief as a season of growing and refinement. But if someone would have told me at the time that's what could come of it, I probably would have told them no thanks, I wasn't interested.

Refinement and growth can be a hard concept to grasp, especially when you are hurting, and it's okay to say that you are not interested. This is a part of the journey that comes in waves and stages. For now, just allow yourself to be open to God's softening of your heart to allow the space needed for His healing.

Chapter 17

The Cobwebs

The home we sold when we moved to China had an attached screened-in porch. The porch was my favorite room in the entire house. It was furnished with big overstuffed comfortable chairs, and the room contained my most favorite feature of all—a water fountain. I love the sound of water, whether it is the ocean, rain or a fountain. Water provides me peace, and God so often speaks to me through it.

Whenever possible, I spent time on that screened-in porch. Every morning I took my Bible and my coffee out to the porch to spend time with God. I created a relaxing ambiance by lighting candles, and as I sat in my comfy chair, God often spoke to me. The natural surroundings helped me to feel more connected to God as water ran through the fountain and the wind blew through the trees and the birds sang in the background. That screened-in porch was my little sanctuary.

My favorite times on the porch were when it rained. I loved listening to the rain falling outside as I read His Word and spent time talking with Him. It was heavenly.

Once we moved back to the States after returning from China, the one thing I hoped for as we searched for a new home was a place with a screened-in-porch. It had been

The Cobwebs

years since we had that type of space, and it was one of the things I missed the most while we lived in China.

I was so excited when we walked into what is now our current home and saw the three-season room off the back of the house. We didn't have much money, but I was able to scrape together enough extra cash to purchase two chairs and a small table for the room. And the icing on the cake? I found a fountain on clearance to complete my little sanctuary – thank you, Father!

Every morning, I headed out to the three-season room armed with my coffee and my Bible, ready to spend time with God. One morning I opened the blinds that led to the porch, and I was shocked at what I found. Behind the blinds along the sliding door, cobwebs filled the space. Everything was covered including the windows and the furniture. It was as if it were a one-hundred-year-old house that had not been lived in for ages. The odd thing about it was that Jim and I had just been out there the previous night and the cobwebs were not there.

I showed Jim my discovery, and he was as dumbfounded as I was. We both thought it was so strange. Jim got a broom and began cleaning off the cobwebs. He had to stop and clean off his broom several times because the cobwebs were so extensive. After he was done, I went out and continued with my morning as usual.

The next morning, I opened the blinds and guess what I discovered? You got it! The cobwebs were back, only this time they were even thicker than those from the day before. Once again, Jim cleaned everything up for me and all was well again.

As for the following morning? You guessed it. The cobwebs were there again. This back and forth went on for over a week!

Experiencing God in THE HIDDEN PLACE

One day I was sitting on the porch when something caught my eye. I looked over and saw a spider about the size of a dime. I went to get a closer look because I thought he might be on the outside of the screen. Sure enough, he wasn't. He was on the inside of the screen.

Now common sense should have told me to get it, but I didn't. He was small, and after living in the deep country woods as we had done for so many years, a spider that size was no big deal to me.

Several days later I saw that silly spider again on the inside of the screen. I figured he was struggling to find his way out, so I decided to help him along. I got a small jar, captured him and released him in the yard.

Well dummy me, I did not put two and two together. Being the country girl that I am, you would have thought that I figured out what was going on. But the next morning I opened the door expecting to find the cobwebs and guess what? Not a single cobweb to be found. (I know, I know, I'm pretty slow on the draw.)

That tiny little spider was the culprit of our daily mess. Who would have thought a spider as small as he was would be capable of making such a mess of webs like that?

As I sat there drinking my coffee, I continued to think about that little spider's cobwebs, and God started to reveal something to me.

How many times had there been cobwebs in my own life that I tried to clean up, or maybe thought I had cleaned up, only for them to return? Maybe they didn't return the very next day, the very next week or even the very next year, but eventually, they would come back rearing their ugly head, and each time I was shocked that they still existed.

The only way to avoid this from happening is not to clean up the cobwebs rather it's to discover the source of

The Cobwebs

the mess - in this case, the spider. What spider is causing such a mess? With this realization, I asked God, "Is this what you're trying to show me? If so, what is my spider?" It was with that simple question that He whispered to my heart, "Trust."

In that moment, I knew God had just revealed a very big piece of the hard, lumpy soil of my soul that needed plowed up.

I had to learn to trust Him again, but the trust needed to look much different than it had in the past. I trusted the calling God had placed on my life. I had said yes to obey whatever He asked me to do.

But now He was calling me to trust Him in the "no." This "no" had the appearance of unanswered prayers, but in reality, He was answering me.

When I cried out to God to save our children, I cried out only willing to accept a very specific answer to that cry. I was not willing to accept His ultimate decision. Instead, I argued with Him because His decision of "no" didn't make sense in my mind. I knew it was not His will for the children to suffer, yet He did nothing to stop it.

When He called us to care for those children, we didn't mind selling our home and giving away our possessions. Our eagerness to obey Him gave us a sense of peace and willingness to leave our home, job, friends, and families. We loved serving Him and caring for orphans on the other side of the world. But when the government changed their policy and our application to continue the work was denied, that's when things started to get confusing.

We knew we had obeyed the law. We did everything we were asked to do. We told the truth. We lived above reproach. But the outcome resulted in losing all our children. The doors were closed, and our family was sent back to

America. I could trust Him in the "yes", but I could not trust Him in the "no". Why was that?

As God began working on my heart in The Hidden Place, He helped me to see that the reason I could trust Him in the yes, but not in the no, was because the yes had such a beautiful result. Orphans were given a home filled with love. Many lives were changed and even saved. Most of our children were adopted by their forever families. The yes all made sense.

The no, however, did not. Our children were now sentenced back to their prisons of suffering, while our family had no home, no job, and no money. Nothing about the no made sense. How could I trust His no when there wasn't anything beautiful about it?

Trust – my spider – was the source of all the cobwebs in my heart. Until I captured that spider it would continue to clutter the sanctuary of my heart. However, capturing a spider so entangled in webs isn't as easy as scooping it into a jar and releasing it in the yard. I had work to do, and it was finally time to get started.

Chapter 18
Half-Truths And Collateral Damage

Half-truths. That was one of the first lessons God taught me about my spider of trust.

The book of Job is a story about a man who loses everything – his wealth, children and health – after God gives Satan permission to take it all away from Job. Job goes on to lament deeply, and eventually, Job's friends chime in with their theories as to why Job is suffering so greatly.

My favorite part of the whole story is what happens after everybody has voiced their opinions about why Job is suffering. God finally had enough of their deliberations, and He begins to speak to Job. Whenever I read this passage, I find myself physically holding onto my seat as God begins, "Brace yourself like a man; I will question you, and you shall answer me." *(Job 38:3)* Gulp! Job was about to receive an earful.

Thinking back to my earlier lament to God, I wondered if God considered having similar words with me to put me in my place. Yet in His grace and mercy, He spared me His wrath and chose a different approach. He knew I was wounded and hurting. He knew how fragile I was, and in The

Hidden Place, He showed me His gentle love, compassion, and understanding, which began to soften my aching heart.

As we look back on the story of Job, God asked Job, "Would you discredit my justice? Would you condemn me to justify yourself?" (Job 40:8) Oh, dear. That question hit the inner core of my being.

When I was questioning God, I felt justified in all my questions and accusations. I was hurt. I couldn't understand what was going on, and I needed answers to help make sense of everything that had happened. My spider - my lack of trust – stemmed from half-truths. Here's what I mean by that.

Half-truths sounds like an oxymoron, I know, but they exist. They are based on your knowledge and experience in a situation. Half-truths become the lens in which you view circumstances and situations. If a little girl grows up being abused by her father, she might reach adulthood believing that all men are abusive. Was she abused? Yes, that is the truth. Are all men abusive? No, that is the lens by which she views men thus establishing a truth that doesn't allow for the whole picture.

Job had no idea that his story started with Satan approaching God. Job didn't know that Satan asked to unleash evil onto Job's family, possessions and health. Job did not know what he did not see. Job had postured himself toward God based on what he could see with only his human eyes.

Do you remember my story about the roaring lion and the battle of light and dark? Do you remember how I shared that God spoke to me and said that the battle was His?

God was revealing truth to my heart, and it was time that I heard it. Through the vision of the roaring lion, God revealed to me the truth that there is so much more going on in the unseen world that we will ever know. He has shown me that not only are we unable to see, but also that our human minds cannot understand all the mysteries of God and His ways.

The mysteries of His ways are vast. A missing child – some are found, while others are never to be seen again. A person with cancer - some are cured, while others die. A couple going through infertility – some conceive, while others don't. A broken marriage – some are restored, while others divorce. A rebellious child – some return safely home, while others never do.

The questions of why will always be a part in this sin-filled world. You do not know the answers; you only know the half-truths – the results of the situation based on the known outcomes.

If you are going to keep your faith in God, you must trust Him because He is the only one who knows the whole and complete truth.

In 2002 there was a movie that came out starring Arnold Schwarzenegger called, "Collateral Damage." Now short of "Kindergarten Cop," I am not a huge Schwarzenegger fan. But this particular movie stuck with me.

In the movie, Schwarzenegger plays a family man who goes to meet his wife and son one afternoon. Schwarzenegger's character sees his family sitting outside on the terrace of a business building having lunch. As he walks over to meet them, they wave happily to greet him. At that moment there is an explosion. Schwarzenegger's character watches as his wife and son are killed in the sudden explosion.

He later learns that his family was killed by a terrorist bomb set off by a Columbian drug ring. He grows frustrated with the official investigation and decides to take matters into his own hands. He takes off for Columbia to hunt down the man who destroyed his family.

Once he finally finds the man, he asks him one question, "Why? My wife and son were innocent. They had nothing to do with your war." The man's answer to Schwarzenegger - they were simply collateral damage.

While this may sound like a cop-out to the many injustices in this world, there is truth to it. Our children, who are still laying in orphanage cribs, are the collateral damage of the evil that is taking place in that country. Those babies are innocent and have done nothing to deserve the injustice and suffering that is happening to them, and yet they suffer anyway.

Collateral damage is a part of the world we live in and it has been since sin first entered the world.

Because this can be such a difficult idea to wrap our minds around, I'd like to share something with you. Do you know the story of Joshua? Joshua was chosen by God to replace Moses as the leader of the Israelites after Moses passed away. Joshua loved God. He was faithful and obedient to everything God asked of him.

The first city that the Israelites took under Joshua's leadership was the City of Jericho. The story goes that Joshua and his men circled the city seven times just as God instructed them to do, after which the walls surrounding the city crumbled.

God gave Joshua some very specific instructions on what he was to do after this victory. They were to destroy everything, while all the silver, gold and articles of bronze and iron were to be put in the treasury – God's treasury.

Why do you think God wanted these items? Think about it. He's God. He doesn't need any worldly treasures. Scripture doesn't tell us why God asked Joshua to do this,

Half-Truths And Collateral Damage

but whatever the reason, what we do know is that Joshua did exactly what God asked. Joshua was given victory over Jericho. Afterwards, Joshua followed God's instructions to destroy everything while placing those specific items into God's treasury.

Soon after, Joshua and the Israelites were called into another battle. This time it was the City of Ai. However, in this battle, God's people were defeated, and Joshua's men were killed. What on earth was going on?

Can you imagine Joshua's confusion? Nothing made sense. He was obedient in everything God asked him to do, both in Jericho and in Ai. Here is where the half-truth comes into play.

Joshua assessed the situation on what he knew and experienced as his truth. He had been obedient and followed every order God had given him in both battles. So then why two different outcomes?

What Joshua didn't know was that after the victory over Jericho, one of Joshua's men, Achan, had kept some of the plunder for himself. Achan later confessed to Joshua that he had taken it and buried it in the ground in his tent.

While Joshua did not know or see this happen, God did. Joshua knew only half of the truth, while God knew the whole truth.

The collateral damage was that Joshua's soldiers, innocent men who had obeyed God, lost their lives. Women lost their husbands and became widows, and children lost their fathers and became fatherless.

The answer to our *why* questions are something we all hold: free will. Once Achan decided to disobey, he exercised his free will, putting himself first rather than God. It had no bearing that Joshua and the others had done their part; the free will of one man won, or in this case, lost the battle.

There will be battles you will fight in this life. Some will be lost, and some will be won. Your part of the battle is to trust in God - trust in His sovereignty with the outcome and remember that the battle is His and not yours.

Chapter 19
The Great Reveal

When God created me in my mother's womb, He instilled in me a quality that has appeared in my life ever since I was a little girl. Anytime I witnessed something that seemed wrong, I was determined to do something to make it right.

It didn't matter if it involved someone I knew or not, I was ready to spring into action. If I saw a kid being picked on, I went to their rescue regardless of who the kid was. If I found out that someone cheated on an assignment or test in school, I became outraged. If I saw someone come to school without a coat or with holes in their shoes, you can bet that I was telling my parents about it to make sure that individual received whatever they needed.

Not to mention, I have always been stubborn . . . boy am I stubborn! I never give up, no matter how hard things get. I am, and I always have been, a very stubborn and driven person.

I know that God created me with these qualities because He knew, even before I took my first breath, what He would one day call me to do. These personal traits of mine would become an essential part of the equipping that I would need to walk out the callings He placed on my life.

In the Hidden Place, God started depositing seeds into

what had become the plowed up, fertile soil of my soul. These seeds were planted to grow a new crop of fruit during the next season of my life. With these new seeds deposited, I found myself asking the question, "Could it be that I endured such deep, dark caverns of sorrow and suffering for such a time as this?"

God knew that when He called me away to The Hidden Place I would stay in His Presence for as long as it took me to get to wholeness again.

Despite the silence and loneliness, I began to seek Him for answers, refusing to give up until He gave them to me. Despite the horrors of what I had walked through, I always knew deep down inside of me, even when my heart would lie and tell me otherwise, that I was His child.

I clung to His promise that He would never leave me or forsake me. If I would draw close to Him, He would draw close to me. Even when it didn't feel true, I chose to believe, knowing the time would eventually come when I had received enough healing. Not only would I believe that He would never leave me or forsake me, but I chose to believe that one day, I would feel the truth of that promise once again.

"I tell you, unless a kernel of wheat falls to the ground and dies, it remains only a single seed. But if it dies, it produces many seeds." (John 12:24)

While this journey has been excruciatingly hard, it has provided me rich intimacy with Him in The Hidden Place. Wounded so deeply from the battle of deep loss and suffering, God drew me ever close to him. He scooped me up with His gentle hands and loved me while I spent precious time with Him. In those early days after China, He spoke to my heart's grief in tears rather than words.

Once the season of mourning and lament began to

The Great Reveal

diminish, it was time to transition to a season of healing. Eventually, that season would transition to the next one, a season of growing.

Your Father is so gentle and so loving. He wants to take each of us away to The Hidden Place with Him. He wants to join you in the place where you can be alone with Him in such a quiet, sweet and private setting. He wants time alone with you not to isolate you from the world, but rather to spend time alone with you - just a Father and His child.

I think of my thirty-plus years of marriage to Jim. One of the key components of our marriage has been spending time alone together as a couple. We spend this time in laughter and sometimes in tears. We spend this time in deep and lengthy conversations. It's in these times together that we can just be as one, without the clamor of the outside world, our kids, our jobs, etc. It strengthens our relationship to simply spend time alone together as one being.

That is what The Hidden Place has looked like for me. Once all those outside noises were hushed, I was able to sit quietly with only my Father. It is in that stillness and quiet that you are positioned to receive His love and comfort. When noises have been hushed in that Hidden Place, you can sit quietly with Him. You are positioned to receive His love and comfort, His guidance and His wisdom, His teaching and His equipping. As your mind is finally emptied and quiet, you can hear and receive all that He has for you.

No matter what the battle looks like for you, there is a comfort process to be found in The Hidden Place. Whether it is the death of a spouse or loved one, a health crisis, infidelity, a rebellious child, a divorce, a job loss, a financial crisis, a serious illness or a horrific accident, God desires to bring you comfort. Regardless of the battle, we know that suffering will eventually invite us on its journey; it's only a question of when.

As Christians, we must remember that we are living in a sin-filled world. Every day there is a battle between good and evil. The enemy has one goal and one goal only, and that is to take us out.

As hard as it is to hear this, God doesn't want you to focus on the battle. He wants you to focus on Him. "For My thoughts are not your thoughts, nor are your ways My ways," says the Lord. "For the heavens are higher than the earth, so are My ways higher than your ways, and My thoughts than your thoughts." (Isaiah 55:8-9)

If we are going to walk through this life as His children, we have to come to a moment in life - especially in the suffering - when we are willing to accept the truth that His ways and His thoughts are higher than ours.

Can you declare that you are going to trust him unconditionally? Can you still find a mustard seed of faith even when the mysteries of His ways and His sovereignty are not able to be understood by our human minds? Without this trust, even the smallest step of trust, we are not able to enjoy the full fruits of living the abundant life He has promised for each one of us as His children.

If you'll remember at the very beginning of this book, I shared that I knew I would never know the answers to my questions of *why* this side of heaven.

The lessons learned in The Hidden Place taught me that I had to choose to trust despite all my unanswered questions. In time, I have found that I can indeed choose that trust again. And in God's grace and in His time, He has given me some insight into my seemingly unanswered questions.

About a year after God sent us back to America, things started to shift in China. There was an onslaught

The Great Reveal

of increased persecution of the Chinese Christian people. The persecution began with crosses being removed from their churches, and it escalated to leaders being arrested. Christians were being banned from attending church.

Then there were those foreigners who remained in the country to provide foster care and other services to the orphans. We watched on this side of the world as the events unfolded before our very eyes. A systematic closing of foster homes began swiftly one by one.

It had begun with our ministry, and it was slowly moving throughout the country. In less than one year, almost every single foster program had closed. Hundreds and hundreds of children were taken from their foster families and returned to their orphanages. Within two years, almost all foreign aid for the orphans in China would come to a screeching halt. A mass exodus of foreign volunteers serving in China soon followed.

Once again, God in His mercy and grace pulled back the curtains to allow me to see the mystery of His ways. Did He have to? Absolutely not. But He did anyway. He helped me to see what could have happened had we stayed and continued running our program. There is so much humbleness inside of my soul that makes me question once again. Why? Why have you found favor with your servant? Why have you helped me to see the why behind what we went through, Father? He didn't have to show us, but He did.

Why did God call us over there for two years just to turn around and bring us back? Why was our ministry dripping in His favor with extravagant provisions, then suddenly closed by the hands of evil in a thirty-minute window of time?

Because He knew what we didn't.

He knew the whole truth, while we only knew half of the truth.

Our truth was that we had said "yes" to His calling of serving orphans in China – a calling which we were prepared to do well into our retirement years.

God's truth was that He knew that we had a very short window of time to get children out of the country and adopted into a forever family. He poured out everything imaginable into our ministry.

He poured out His provisions all over us so that we had every single resource needed to carry out His plan in the short amount of time He knew we would be allotted.

In His mercy and grace, He provided me with a physical picture in a newspaper that would give me the assurance that I had done nothing wrong to cause us to lose our babies. Even then, He was pointing me One Way, to Truth.

He knew the feelings of guilt I would experience, thinking that I somehow had caused this to happen. He knew I would need to look back on that paper and feel His comfort and assurance that we did the right thing. He knew where my heart would go, and long before I knew the fullness of the journey He was taking us on, He was protecting me.

In His mercy, He had something even bigger to reveal to me. As things began to get increasingly problematic in China, we believe it would have been unwise to keep our children in the country. Even though they were US citizens, they were still Chinese nationals. If China wanted to cause problems for our family, our children could have been at risk. They easily could have been targeted.

I know with every ounce of certainty in my soul, if I were put into a position in which I was forced to choose to take our foster children back to the orphanage, it would have backed me into a corner.

I do not know if I could have chosen to take our babies back on my own free will.

The Great Reveal

And yet if I did – if I found myself in a position to have to do such a heart-wrenching thing - I know I would have lived with the guilt of that decision for the rest of my life. Absolutely, hands down, I would not have been able to live with myself.

My Father created my heart, and He knows every intricate detail of what makes it tick. He loves me so much, and He has so much mercy for me. Because of that, He was not going to allow me to be put in that situation.

Despite all the pain and sorrow of having our children taken from us, as my loving Father, I now know He protected me.

In the quietness of The Hidden Place, I humbly bowed on my knees with my face pressed into the fresh soil of my soul, and I asked the same question as Ruth, "Why have I found favor in thine eyes?"

Chapter 20
Leaving The Hidden Place

"Therefore, I am now going to allure her; I will lead her into the wilderness and speak tenderly to her. There I will give her back her vineyards and will make the Valley of Achor a door of hope. There she will respond as in the days of her youth; as in the day she came up out of Egypt." (Hosea 2:14-15)

This is the verse God spoke to me as He invited me to go away with Him to The Hidden Place. Now, many seasons later, I can see the many truths within this promise that have been revealed to my heart.

When Achan confessed to Joshua that he stole and hid some of the treasures after the battle of Jericho, Joshua retrieved the items Achan had taken. Joshua had Achan killed for his sin and disobedience. Placed over Achan's burial site is a large pile of rocks which remain there to this day. The place is called the Valley of Achor.

The Valley of Achor symbolizes a time of great heartache and suffering for the Israelites. It serves as a reminder that despite their obedience to God, they were the collateral damage of one man's free will to sin. Joshua lost his men, wives lost their husbands, and children lost their fathers.

But through the prophet Hosea, God promised that He would make the Valley of Achor a *door of hope*.

A door is a means to pass through from one area to another. In these verses, God promises the Israelites that He would lead them from their season of suffering and grief, and transport them through the door to the other side, a new season of hope.

As I sat in my counselor's office, I told her that I wasn't sure if I was writing this book for myself or others. She replied, "Both." I know she was right.

The messages given to me and the lessons my Father taught me in The Hidden Place are not to be kept, but rather, they are to be shared with others who are walking through their own seasons of grief and sorrow.

I believe God wants His message to be shared with His children. As temporary residents of this sin-filled world, we are surrounded by so much evil and sadness. Despite all of this, we are His children and He is our Father.

He wants you to learn how to not only walk through life's hardships, but He also wants you to grow closer to Him as you do. As your loving Father, He is near to you in every moment of your daily life, including the hard parts. It's up to you to have the eyes to see Him.

He lured me into The Hidden Place, not only so that I could rest, but also so I could grieve with Him. So that I would have the time and space needed for Him to quietly love me through my grief.

Once I was ready to hear Him speak, He plowed up the soil of my soul and began to reveal to me all the lessons He wanted to teach me. He has gifted me with His words that bring me into the realm of insight just enough to understand His perfect sovereignty over my life.

In doing all of this, He has graciously given me a sense of sacredness in my suffering.

My posture in The Hidden Place went from face down before Him in mourning, to face down before Him in love, joy, and worship.

The words written in this book were pulled from my journal entries and include many of the conversations we had during our time in The Hidden Place. As I draw closer to the end, I find myself still laying my head across His lap. My tears are no longer tears of sadness, but rather tears of joy, love, and thankfulness for His healing.

My heart is packed full of wonder at His magnificent glory. I am in awe of His extravagant love for me, and His gentle process of bringing me to a place of healing.

A place of hope and new beginnings.

From brokenness to wholeness.

In His goodness I have discovered a place where my soul can once again worship Him, declaring that indeed He is a good, good Father.

My heart and soul now know that no matter what, I can trust Him in the yes and in the no.

He has transported me from grief through the door to the other side - a place of hope and new beginnings. A place of healing. And a place where I have once again found His omnipotent power and infinite wisdom in all things.

My life will forever be changed by the hundreds of children God called me to love and serve. Their faces will forever be etched into my heart. Some have stories that ended happily, while most of them did not.

CLARA – The sweet brown-eyed girl who had to army crawl to reach the toilet, was finally adopted and is now living with her forever family in the US.

Leaving The Hidden Place

CLARA LOVES BALLET³

Clara attends school and lives a full life, filled with love and endless possibilities. She is smart and confident, and she still sports her beautiful, gentle smile that I first saw when she was able to sit up in a chair and play with the other children in the orphanage activity room.

LUCY - The sweet girl who once knew the love of a family until she had been abandoned, remains on the sixth floor of the orphanage. Lucy's mama never did come for her.

LUCY CURRENT DAY IN THE ORPHANAGE

Experiencing God in THE HIDDEN PLACE

Lucy will never be adopted since she has reached the tender age of fourteen, which disqualifies her for legal adoption according to Chinese law.

MARY - Oh, my sweet Mary. She suffered so much because of the condition that caused her fingers and toes to be deformed. I cherish the precious memories we have of Mary, including the wonderful day we spent with her as she experienced the mall and the beach for the very first time. That memory is filled with so much fun and happiness. Little did I know, I would never see Mary again.

After that day at the beach, we were told that Mary's condition had worsened. She is no longer able to feed herself or walk on her own. When we last asked to visit with her, the orphanage staff reported back that she was too embarrassed, and she didn't want to be seen by anyone. She now spends her days confined to her bed. She is unable to walk, and she must be fed by a caregiver.

LAST PICTURE TAKEN OF MARY

My heart still cries whenever I think about Mary. My heart is filled with deep, deep sorrow for her and the hundreds of thousands of other Marys who live out their life sentences as prisoners inside of an orphanage. Orphans who will never experience the love and joy of having a family of their own. I know that God's heart grieves as He witnesses the daily injustice of these children's lives.

MIMI – My sweet and beautiful Mimi. She will forever be the hero of my heart. I can still remember the grueling fight that I endured in getting her to eat. I still remember the way she lit up in my arms when I sang to her, "Jesus Loves Me." She taught me what it means to be brave, and she modeled for me what it can look like to fight for healing and wholeness.

MIMI

Mimi now lives with her forever family in the US. She attends school. She continues to learn how to speak, and she will proudly show off her skills of naming all her shapes and colors when given the chance. She is bright, energetic, and is full of life.

To this day, Mimi's love language is still music. It is not uncommon to find her in the front of the sanctuary of her family's church as she sways and moves to the music. Her arms lifted high as she gets lost in the rhythm of God's love as she worships Him. The God of the Universe who plucked her out of darkness to heal her and make her whole again.

ISABELLA - Despite the heartache and grief of losing our tiny Isabella, the sweet baby with a fatal heart condition, I am so thankful that God allowed me to give her the gift of love. She had a face and a name, and she did not leave this earth as an orphan, rather she left having known and experienced the love of a family. I know Jesus is holding her, and my heart is comforted knowing that she is now whole and healed. I am looking forward to the day we will be reunited in heaven. What a glorious reunion that will be!

VICKIE HOLDING *ISABELLA*

NEIGHBOR – The mama who wanted to give her baby to us stayed in contact even after we had returned to the States. We had our manager visit her frequently to see how both mom and baby were doing. During her visits, our manager would stay for much of the day, keeping Mom company and giving her someone to talk to as she lovingly mothered her baby.

We would chat with mom through China's social media group, and almost daily she would send us pictures of her baby. She was so proud of her baby, and rightfully so. Her baby had chubby arms and legs, and when she smiled, she revealed the biggest dimples. We loved getting daily photos and videos of her.

One day she sent a message. All it said was, "Too much fluid." We knew what this meant. The next day we received a call from our manager confirming what we already suspected, the baby had passed away. Mom had contacted our manager with the tragic news and expressed that she wanted us to know.

NEIGHBOR WITH HER BABY

Despite the sad ending to this story, I was so proud of this mom and her bravery. She did not give in to her family's pressure to abandon her baby. Instead of regret, she now has beautiful memories of holding her baby and loving her until she took her final breath. I think about all the memories she captured through the many photos and videos she took of her daughter. They will be treasures for her to keep forever.

On that dreaded day when the orphanage officials arrived at our home, we lost eighteen children into the hands of evil. Since then, we have been so blessed to have thirteen of them adopted by families from the US. Five of our children remain in the orphanage waiting to be adopted. In honor of those children, here are their names so that you can pray for them: Ben, Cody, Caleb, Hannah, and Faith.

Leaving The Hidden Place

NOAH REUNITED WITH FOSTER AYI AFTER ADOPTION[4]

This is a picture of one of our foster children, Noah. On that fateful day, Noah was one of our children taken from us and returned to the orphanage. A year later he was adopted. His family traveled back to the city of our foster home where Noah was reunited with his ayi who had loved and cared for him. Her expression says it all!

Adoption is such a beautiful exchange of unmerited love and grace, just like our Father gives to us when we are adopted into His forever family. If you are interested in learning more about adoption, either international or domestic, or becoming a foster parent in your local county, you can find many resources through the Christian Alliance for Orphans at www.cafo.org

As for our organization, with our foster care program, we had two foster homes which were only in operation for nineteen months. In total, we cared for thirty-three babies.

Twenty-seven of which were adopted, and one passed into the hands of Jesus.

During our decade long ministry, we provided specialized infant nurture care to over three hundred children. We had a preschool program for special needs children which served close to one hundred children. We provided medical care, educational assistance, summer camps, life skills training, and mentorship programs to the hundreds of children and teens who were growing up in the orphanage.

We estimate through the efforts of our organization, over five hundred children were advocated for and adopted. Hundreds more were served and benefited from our programs.

I don't share all of that to brag, but rather to serve as a testimony to the mighty God that we serve. We give Him all the glory and praise Him with what He will do with our simple "yes" when He calls on us.

As for our family, we continue to live in Ohio, raising our four younger children, while keeping up with our three grown children and their families.

For me personally, God has shown me that my mission is the same today as it was all those years ago, sitting in that hotel room on the other side of the world. To help bring hope and healing to those who are broken and wounded.

The time I spent in The Hidden Place forever changed my life. Before entering The Hidden Place, I thought I knew God, but it wasn't until I actually experienced Him in such an intimate way that I now have a better understanding of what trust in His Word and in His Ways really look like.

I now understand that while we are all called to be His Hands and His Feet on this earth, more than anything He desires our love and a relationship with Him.

I now understand that just because He works good in all things, does not mean all things are good.

I now understand that He wants us, His children, to come to Him and seek Him with all our questions. Whether you are suffering or dealing with injustice, whether you are seeking wisdom or dealing with a question on your heart.

I now understand that God desires us to go with Him to The Hidden Place to be with Him to worship, to rest, and even just to be still in His Presence.

Being with God in The Hidden Place allows you to be wide open and exposed to His love, His Wisdom and His understanding.

Our King. Our God. Our Savior. Our Father.

You will never be fully capable of understanding His mysterious ways, yet when you choose to trust Him in everything, you will experience a depth of peace and an intimate love that only God can provide you when you are in a relationship with Him. And from that trust comes hope.

I wait with great anticipation for the day when all the battles of good and evil have been fought and the war is finally over. And in case you are wondering who wins, it's already been determined. All you have to do is read the end of The Book.

When all the battles have been fought and God has declared His final victory over the war, you will sit at His feet and He will wipe every tear from your eyes. There will be no more death, no more mourning, no more suffering and no more pain.

Hallelujah and Amen!

"And I heard a loud voice from the throne saying, 'Look! God's dwelling place is now among the people, and he will dwell with them. They will be his people, and God himself will be with them and be their God. He will wipe every tear from their eyes. There will be no more death or mourning or crying or pain, for the old order of things has passed away'

He who was seated on the throne said, 'I am making everything new!' Then he said, 'Write this down, for these words are trustworthy and true.'

He said to me: 'It is done. I am the Alpha and the Omega, the Beginning and the End. To the thirsty, I will give water without cost from the spring of the water of life. Those who are victorious will inherit all this, and I will be their God and they will be my children.'" (Rev. 21:3-7)

A closing note from Vickie:

The words, "Thank you" do not seem adequate right now. But seriously, thank you.

Thank you for allowing me to share my heart with you and thank you for trusting me with yours by coming along with me.

As I shared early on, I will never proclaim to be an expert, but my hope was if I could share with you some of the lessons God taught me, and the steps He had me take in my healing journey, that it could be used to help others.

As I walked through this healing journey, God taught me a very important lesson. "Yes," God's ways and thoughts are mysterious. "Yes," there will be times that you will not be able to understand them. But, one thing that is not mysterious or hard to understand is God's love for you. He makes that very simple.

God loves you and He desires to be in a relationship with you. In return, He wants you to love Him and be in a relationship with Him.

It really is that simple.

Out of that loving relationship comes a beautiful thing called trust.

And from trusting Him comes the one thing you need to walk out your days in this sin-filled world. Hope.

Trusting in Him brings Hope.

Hope for healing.

Hope for new life and new beginnings

In Him lies the door of hope. All you need to do is walk through it.

If you have never accepted Jesus as your personal savior, or if you are unsure of your hope in spending eternity with

Him in heaven, you can whisper this simple prayer right now. He's waiting.

"Father, thank you for loving me and sending your son Jesus to die as a sacrifice for my sins. I know that I am a sinner and ask for your forgiveness. I accept you as my personal savior. Thank you for loving me and desiring to have me as your child. Amen"

Never forget that you are His and that no person or situation can ever change that security. He loves you. You can trust Him. In the yes and in the no.

Live in the assurance and freedom that hope brings to you each day!

In His Grip,

Vickie

Endnotes

1 Photo credit, Kirsti Mutz-Lewis, People Like Us
2 Illustration by Artist, Andrew Wesley Bennett
3 Photo credit, Diane Feldt/Bob Gregory
4 Photo credit, Valerie Martin

About the Author

At the age of 40, Vickie and her husband boarded a plane for China to adopt a baby girl. What started as a journey of adoption, ended in a decade long ministry of serving the orphans of China.

Vickie loves sharing stories about the children she served, her wild and crazy adventures while living in China, and how God taught her heart the power of His love, compassion, and healing for a wounded and broken spirit.

Vickie will weave scriptures and Bible teachings throughout her stories as she ministers to those who are either walking through a hard journey or struggling with their identity and God's love for them.

Vickie is a speaker, Bible teacher, adoption advocate, and trainer. She is the Co-founder and Director of two organizations that served orphans in China.

Vickie is married to her soul mate, Jim. They have seven children and one very spoiled dog. Vickie's favorite thing to do is awake early in the morning, with coffee in hand, to spend time alone with God. She loves to read, travel, and spend time with her girlfriends chatting over a cup of coffee.

www.vickiebennett.org

CPSIA information can be obtained
at www.ICGtesting.com
Printed in the USA
BVHW030820050620
580960BV00001B/9